THE
BACK-IN-YOUR-FACE
GUIDE TO
PICK-UP BASKETBALL

We're running it back—back in your face. (Budd Symes)

THE
BACK-IN-YOUR-FACE
GUIDE TO
PICK-UP BASKETBALL

*A Have-Jump-Shot, Will-Travel Tour
of America's Hoops Hotspots*

CHUCK WIELGUS AND
ALEXANDER WOLFF

ILLUSTRATED BY N. E. WOLFF

Dodd, Mead & Company
New York

Published by Dodd, Mead & Company, Inc.
79 Madison Avenue, New York, N.Y. 10016
Distributed in Canada by
McClelland and Stewart Limited, Toronto
Manufactured in the United States of America
Designed by Kingsley Parker
First Edition

1 2 3 4 5 6 7 8 9 10

Library of Congress Cataloging-in-Publication Data

Wielgus, Chuck.
  The back-in-your-face guide to pick-up basketball.

  Continues The in-your-face basketball book, c1980.
  1. Basketball—United States.   2. Playgrounds—
United States.   I. Wolff, Alexander, 1957–
II. title.
GV885.7.W5   1986   796.32′3′0973   86-6348
ISBN 0-396-08709-4 (pbk.)

To Chris and Leslie, for understanding and
supporting this passion; and Chip and Tom,
that they may have the opportunity and
determination to pursue their dreams.

"Say, where'd you learn to dunk, in finishing school? Dunking's an art!"

—Clark Gable to Claudette Colbert
in *It Happened One Night*

CONTENTS

CONTENTS

A BEHIND-THE-BACK PASS
TO . . .

There is no way to credit all the assists in a project like this. The uncountable hundreds who chipped in information, courts, and pictures will have to make do with the same sort of satisfaction a good dish gives you on the playground.

We must, however, acknowledge by name Joe Dean and Al Harden of Converse, for their confidence and support; the Navy's Pat Millea, who fatigues his fatigues with all the hoop he plays; Hank Hersch, Frank Dell'Apa, Charlie Pierce, Brian Brattebo, Tom Schneider, Fran McCaffery and Detlef Schrempf, for their exceptional assistance; Dick (Hoops) Weiss, for *his* assistance—and for being, like us, so shamelessly proud of his depravity; Larry Donald, Ray Frager, Rita Napolitano, and the inimitable Gus Macker, for helping us put out an APB for submissions; Jeff Blumb, for his skill both in staging Bookstore and communicating its essence; Tom Konchalski, for sharing with us the fruits of being the most passionate and knowledgeable worm in the Apple; Mark Bradley, for his poop on Pretty Pie and hats (or lack of them); Steve Fine, Eric Godwin, and Tricia Wall, for helping us get the big picture; the personnel at the state parks and recreation associations of Alaska, Illinois, Indiana, Kansas, Montana, New Hampshire, Oklahoma, South Carolina, and Vermont, for canvassing their membership on our behalf; the innumerable in-the-field professionals at colleges, YMCAs, and parks and recreation departments who responded to our questionnaires and phone calls; Mark Mulvoy and John Papanek, Alex's editors at *Sports Illustrated,* for helping him make time to pursue this project; Evan Marshall, for his representation; and Jerry Gross, for his editorial guidance. Jerry claimed to be Blanche DuBois on the wrong streetcar, but his instincts were as streetwise as they could be.

In addition, the many fine photographers who clicked their shutters on our behalf deserve to be dealt digits, and Ed Burns, Nicholas Dawidoff, and Katherine Wolff all provided valuable assistance when we needed it most.

And the book simply would not have been finished without the help of our research associates, Mike McCollow and Steve Rushin. It got so we felt we were locked in a game of two-on-two with them, a run none of us wanted to end. May they J every day of their lives.

New York City
January 1986

xi

Since IYF we've stopped and popped at some of the best spots from coast to coast . . . (Blake Discher)

PRE-FACE

Soon after we'd had a good run writing *The In-Your-Face Basketball Book* several years ago, we started getting letters. These letters led us to believe we'd struck a nerve.

A couple of law students at the University of Virginia drove coast to coast, with a ball in their trunk and *IYF* as a Baedeker, and wrote of their odyssey for Long Island's *Newsday*. An expatriate New Yorker who hitchhiked cross-country in the early '70s, his rock in his backpack, told us of the gym in his adopted home, Leadville, Colorado, elevation 10,125—as good a place as any from which to "talk to God." A self-styled "Dawk-a-Holic" described how she trolled the playgrounds of Cleveland, stalking new talent on the order of Darryl Dawkins. A Los Angeleno named Basketball Sam sent us his business card with its inscription, HAVE MOVES, WILL PLAY.

Doctors and lawyers confided in us their obsessions, proving positively that there's more to being goal-oriented than meets the eye. One Boston barrister—he's known as El Blanco on the largely Hispanic Hub playground he frequents—detailed how he has indulged his vice in places as far-flung as Mexico and Paris, where he had a regular run with West African students. "You have no idea," wrote El Blanco, "how weird it is playing with black guys who can't jump."

From Georgia, Matt (The Kid) Williamson weighed in with a paean to Augusta's Warren Road (The Road) Community Center. When Irvin Holley and his buddy Dwight Hinton hook up at Wing Park in Elgin, Illinois, Irvin wrote, they'll challenge each other with, "Let's remap the heavens." And Arthur Filmore gushed over a 5'9" high schooler named Philip Liebschutz, a frequenter of the Solomon Schechter Day School in Malden, Massachusetts, who "should go on to be a college star and eventually grace the pros with his powerful presence." *Philip Liebschutz?*

There were, however, other letters. Angry letters. Letters of reproach. Letters of chastisement. Letters of up*braid*ment. Letters that went, more or less, like this: "Whereas J. J. (Mother) Shipp Rec Center has the baddest dudes in the world, who throw it down on even the Doctor if he shows up some fine summer's day, howzit you chumps don't give it no pub?" Stuff like that.

Having no adequate riposte to the senders of these missives, except that we did our damnedest to put together a representative sample of

. . . and really gotten after it . . . (Budd Symes)

. . . *to be able to come at you with* Son of Face. *(Joe Traver)*

100 or so of the finest courts in the nation for *IYF*, we've taken steps to rectify the oversights. If no pub's your rub, if you wanted more poop on more places, in particular *your* place, than *IYF* supplied, we've aimed (off the glass, when necessary) to please. *BIYF* features more than 500 hoopsters' havens, from Caribou to Honolulu. We've highlighted worthy indoor spots as well as outdoor ones. (The dude with the severe jones plays through a monsoon; the *smart* dude with the severe jones sneaks into the Y when the ugly clouds roll in.) And for each court we've added new symbols that out-Michelin *IYF*, symbols that tell you the important stuff, like: the kind of racial distribution you can expect, how rough the play gets, where to tune your box.

Some English dude once told a foreign visitor that to learn more about the culture he found so alien, he'd do well to examine Brits at play. ''By our games you shall know us,'' he uttered, or words to that effect. See if you can't get a sense of the texture of America as you follow us following the bouncing ball. We couldn't help but notice how New Yorkers, ever suspicious, not only don't pass, but take the rock right to the rack. How wholesome Hoosiers play their clean, crisp, pass-and-shoot game without half-court ''make it, take it,'' for they need no artificial incentive to play defense. How the improvisatory, free-for-all warm-up game of 21 is so popular throughout the rural, gutbucket South. And how mellow Californians will play laid-back half court—but with a three-seconds rule. After all, property values are high.

As we shook-and-baked in Salt Lake, and yelled ''down'' in Chitown, and played ourselves silly in Philly, we were alarmed at the number of times we found NO DUNKING stenciled on backboards. But, ultimately, we were heartened by how often a basketball broke the ice, especially in neighborhoods that seemed strange to us, and in which we no doubt seemed stranger still.

Enough already. With *IYF* we were only just breaking a sweat. Since then, with ears pressed to the pavement, we've taken notes when not taking jumpers, and fired off questionnaires when not firing off outlet passes, and gotten on the horn when not getting around the rim, to put together what you hold in your hands. We hatched the idea for *The In-Your-Face Basketball Book* over a lunchtime game of H-O-R-S-E; *The Back-in-Your-Face Guide to Pick-up Basketball,* by contrast, was a reflexive act of self-defense. But it was no less a labor of love.

We're down for another. C'mon and run with us.

USE US

We've refined the reference symbols we introduced in *IYF* to provide poop on each site listed. We've also added a number of new symbols, and you'll find each court tagged with several sentences designed to impart anything about a facility that symbols alone won't do justice to. As a result, you ought to be able to step onto the wood at more than 500 places around the country and fit in like a regular homeboy.

OUTDOORS

We'll admit it: we're biased in favor of hoops *al fresco*. Where these rays appear, you can play ball in the open air.

HOOPS AND SLABS

6/3

The first figure tells you how many baskets are standing tall; the second, how many full courts exist as a result. Where the second figure isn't half of the first, you'll know that a half-court or warm-up hoop is on site.

RACK AND TWINE

 Level rim with net

 Level rim without net

 Bent rim with net

 Bent rim without net

The trend around the land is unmistakable and encouraging: more and more rings have string. Rims are also more likely to be level. Neither of these developments, we hasten to add, is the result of dudes hangin' on 'em any less, or hangin' out any less. More likely, the authorities are simply more willing to maintain courts that get used. And more power to 'em. Just the same, the condition of the goal is something you'll want to be aware of.

WHERE IT'S AT

 Urban

 Suburban, shorefront, or campus

 Small town or rural

Needless to say, you won't find many wooden backboards among the metropolitan New York listings, or too many perforated metal ones in the Dakotas. Still, the assignment of these boards is hardly cut-and-dried, and there's the occasional surprise. For instance, the court alongside Lake Michigan on Chicago's Farwell Avenue is but an assist away from the beach at Harrigan Park. The atmosphere, however, is decidedly citified, so we've graced its listing with an urban board. Similarly, we bestowed a wooden board, not the campus fan you might expect, on Martin-Brock Gym at Emory & Henry College. The reason: there's a hayseed spirit to the ball played at this vest-pocket school in southwestern Virginia.

BEST COMP

 Occasional pro or top-flight college

 Average college or top-flight high school

 Average high school or recreational adult

 Junior high or hacker

When you've vested yourself with the power of a fickle restaurant critic, capable of making or breaking a place with a single review, you have to give the matter of a court's competition rating your most considered thought. We were unimpressed with tales about *ex*-pros runnin' at a spot if no current stud-horses did. (What have you done for us *lately*?) We didn't downgrade a place just because we got in a bad run during one visit, provided we saw evidence that the *best* comp you could find there—after all, that's what this symbol means—might have shown up some other day. As you might expect, most sites fall into the middle two categories, somewhere between high schoolers and recreational adults at one end of the scale and college types at the other. And while a few spots earn a leather, high-top Con as a top-of-the-line facility, our compilation (and fun) wouldn't be complete without recognizing the occasional hacker's haven. Shake your booty.

GOTTA WIN BY TWO

On some courts, you don't win 'til you're up by two, *à la* deuce in tennis. Other places—especially those where courts are so heavily used that games can't be dragged out—hew to "straight," where you win "when you get there." Consider the deuce symbol forewarning that you may be in for a long game, or a long wait.

MAKE IT, TAKE IT

Where this symbol appears, "winner's out" prevails in half-court games. That is, you keep the ball as long as you keep scoring. Where the symbol doesn't appear, possession reverts to the defense after a basket, just as in any full-court game.

WORKING LIGHTS

Where an outdoor court features the Edisonian ideogram, illumination can prolong play another several hours. And when you see this symbol next to a court in a hot-weather clime (Phoenix's Encanto Park, for instance, or Miami's Tamiami Park), you can be pretty sure that the best ball takes place at night.

REFRESHMENTS

Working water fountain nearby. It may not be essential, but it sure is nice. If there's none, check out the tag line, where we may have an alternative beverage recommendation.

WOMEN

Women play often. Even where this symbol does appear, women probably don't play often enough. For some reason, pick-up play has yet to catch on on the distaff side. Instead, girls prefer more organized scenarios, like summer leagues, when they wanna have fun.

xix

LEAGUE PLAY

The whistle indicates that a summer or winter league or tournament goes down here, in addition to pick-up. Winter loops tend to be clannish, social things: hoops among friends, with postgame pizza and beer. Summer leagues, by contrast, usually have atmosphere to go with the competition. As more and more receive NCAA sanction, their quality has increased. From the Smith League in Buffalo, to the Riverfront League in Tampa, to the cross-cultural experience to be had in Venice Beach, California, you'll find hoops a happening.

ROUGH PLAY

If exceptional pushing and shoving is the norm, we've so noted with this symbol. Consider the glove our suggestion not to call any touch fouls, and to review your life-insurance policy before taking the court.

RACIAL MIX

Salt stands for whites; pepper for blacks. If only one shaker appears, that race predominates. By including this info, we're in no way endorsing the epidermal status quo, or intending to dissuade anyone of *any* hue from strutting his or her stuff anywhere. On the contrary, your game is a sort of passport: if it's "valid," so to speak, you'll be accepted. And we've made a point of not including any place where any sort of hatred is going down. In fact, if more white dudes sought out pepper places, and more bros took their games to salty locales, the world would be . . . you know what we're saying.

ON YOUR DIAL

Anyone hip to hoop knows that music and ball go hand-in-hand—ball in one hand, box in the other. In making our over-the-air recommendations, we've tried to choose stations that reflect both the community and the court's regular clientele, not just our tastes. (Those tastes, we'll admit, run toward R&B; you haven't lived until you've played ball to Total Control, 96.3 FM, in Albany, Georgia.) You won't, for instance, find us touting a soft-rock station for Detroit's St. Cecilia Church Gym. Or a station that plays Motley Crüe for the Fieldhouse at BYU. Where a local hip-hop artist provides live patter, we've duly noted so in the tag line.

Every court has its own code of conduct. (Heinz Kluetmeier)

ALABAMA

ZINN PARK
14TH AND GURNEE
ANNISTON, ALABAMA

 2/1   1450 AM

A town square of sorts, with a civic ambience. Leagues play out of the community centers. A more residential run takes place over at Lincoln Park.

SLAM BAM, THANK YOU 'HAM

Could Randy Newman have been serenading hoops when he mumbled "Birmingham, Birmingham, the greatest city in Alabam' "? If it is number 1, it's in spite of the efforts of the Birmingham City Council, which recently adopted an ordinance banning basketball from the city's streets. Still, in a state where they genuflected at a football coach named Bear, and where his hoops counterpart for years has been a guy named Wimp, there's no suppressing the ball-bouncing public. Birmingham has risen above all pettiness to become, next to Memphis, the South's ball-playing capital. Each of The Ham's sixteen municipal rec centers provides plenty of free-play time, and the local summer league, which runs out of UAB's Bell Gym, is good enough to keep Charles Barkley, the Round Mound of Rebound, reasonably svelte.

ENSLEY PARK REC CENTER
2800 AVENUE K
BIRMINGHAM, ALABAMA

 2/1   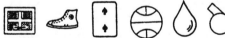   1400 AM

For a full-court run, come by any weekday between noon and 3. On Fridays all the coal miners show. Don't let them give you the shaft.

HAWKINS PARK REC CENTER
8920 ROEBUCK
BIRMINGHAM, ALABAMA

4/2

Primarily half-court here, but when the junior college types choose to come 'round, things get stretched out.

JUDGE ROY BEAN COURT
HIGHWAY 98 (SCENIC ROUTE)
DAPHNE, ALABAMA

 1/0

This dirt court, with its single hoop up on a pine tree, gets intense use on Sunday afternoons. Bean is a public tavern, where Willie Nelson and Jimmy Buffett have done a different sort of playing. ''Lotta H-O-R-S-E,'' says the proprietor, ''or any word you wanna use.''

Dapne *The honky-tonk ball at Judge Roy Bean's court gets gaveled to order on Sunday afternoons.*

WALTON PARK
ROCKY BRANCH
DOTHAN, ALABAMA

6/3

In spite of the name, there aren't any fair-skinned redheads to be found here. One more outdoor slab awaits you over on Lake, at the Lincoln Community Center.

TEXAS STREET AREA REC CENTER
TEXAS AND SELMA
MOBILE, ALABAMA

4/1   92.9 FM

You get "down" on the chalkboard before taking to the tile floor. It's closed weekends, so show up Tuesday and Thursday for best runs. And it's one of the city's few air-conditioned rec centers, so don't be dissuaded from showing in the summer. A more adult crowd hangs out at the Dearborn Street Y.

BELLINGRATH COMMUNITY CENTER
WEST EDGEMONT AND GOODE
MONTGOMERY, ALABAMA

6/3   1600 AM

Gotta get on the supervisor's list to get in a game here, or face banishment to one of three full slabs outside. Like all of the capital city's community centers, Bellingrath is linked to a junior high, stays open almost every night, and is most active during the winter and fall.

OXFORD CIVIC CENTER
MCCULLARS
OXFORD, ALABAMA

6/3   1450 AM

They call the main game here "quarter court"—a sort of vest-pocket full court, played four-on-four at the side baskets.

CLAUDE BROWN YMCA
1133 MINTER
SELMA, ALABAMA

6/3

There's lots of free-play time, though at $1 a pop—pay as you play— the "free" part's a misnomer. The winter league is more exclusive than its summer counterpart. We've declined to recommend a radio station because tunage rotates among three different frequencies, we're told, "to promote community happiness."

BRYCE FIELD
UNIVERSITY OF ALABAMA
TUSCALOOSA, ALABAMA

 4/2

Brothers of both the orthodox and fraternity persuasions are in evidence here. The more serious siblings take their act to Memorial Coliseum.

THE PARK
BASKIN
UNION SPRINGS, ALABAMA

 2/1

The Park? *Yup. Unfortunately, The Lights have never worked. The Shade, as provided by a pleasant courtside stand of trees, is more reliable.*

ALASKA

MINNESOTA PARK
MINNESOTA AND WEST 36TH
ANCHORAGE, ALASKA

  4/2    101.3 FM

Who needs lights? You can bop 'til you drop during the white nights in these parts. This spot, by a major thoroughfare, is the first one to check out; then cruise the court at Fish Creek Park, which is a little more bucolic.

UAA SPORTS CENTER
UNIVERSITY OF ALASKA
ANCHORAGE, ALASKA

6/3    101.3 FM

The noon-hour pick-up during the academic year is a.k.a. the Great Alaska Shootout. The day's quickest moves are often made in the rush to get on the first-sign, first-play list.

MOUNT JUMBO GYM
4TH AND D
DOUGLAS, ALASKA

2/1    630 AM

The worthy regulars at the Juneau Volunteer Fire Dept. ventured to this suburb and renovated the gym. It gets a lot of use, and has generated plenty of civic pride.

5

SCHOERBAR JUNIOR HIGH GYM
SCHOERBAR
KETCHIKAN, ALASKA

6/3   105.9 FM

Even if beer in these parts goes for $2 a can, and the clientele is on the slow, heavy, and pale side, the three-on-three's free, three nights a week.

REAL PICK-UP BALLPLAYERS . . .

DON'T	*DO*
• Drive Saab Turbos	• Drive Cordobas
• Listen to Lionel Richie	• Listen to Cameo
• Tune Al McGuire out	• Tune Billy Packer out
• Care what Dick Vitale has to say about Pearl Washington	• Care what Pearl Washington has to say about Dick Vitale
• Give themselves nicknames	• Answer to nicknames bestowed on them
• Wear Reebok running shoes	• Wear high-tops with street clothes
• Order from L. L. Bean	• Order from drive-thru windows
• Drink beverages with Nutra-Sweet	• Drink orange or grape soda
• Pop when they can drive	• Use the exact-change lane
• Call offensive fouls	• Leave their man to help on D
• Give it up on a two-on-one	• Give it up on a three-on-two
• Drink wine	• Drink malt liquor
• Name their son Hugo	• Name their son Martel
• Try to dunk in a game when they can't	• Try to dunk at game point
• Name their daughter Grace	• Name their daughter anything beginning with "La" (Lavette, LaTanya, LaNancy, etc.)
• Show at the park wearing a Walkman	• Show at the park with a box
• Decline a spot in the next game because they're "tired"	• Shoot for a spot in the next game, regardless of how many runs they've had

ARIZONA

YOUTH CENTER
2403 NORTH ISABEL
FLAGSTAFF, ARIZONA

 2/1   690 AM

If you don't find stardom here, check out the nearby Lowell Observatory, where you may catch a glimpse of Lovetron. Or check out Gogbill, indoors, where they go half court.

ENCANTO PARK SPORTS COMPLEX
15TH AND ENCANTO
PHOENIX, ARIZONA

 6/3   94.5 FM

The most welcome by-product of the park's redevelopment in 1984 is these courts, which are part of a racquetball/tennis/volleyball cluster. This may be the pick-up spot closest to an NBA arena; the Suns play two blocks away.

HERMOSA PARK
20TH AND SOUTHERN
PHOENIX, ARIZONA

 2/1   1060 AM

Lights are de rigueur in these parts. Even the Suns who frequent this spot know the ball is no-shake, all-bake on many days. The city's most ethnic run.

ACTIVITY CENTER
GURLEY AND SHELDON
PRESCOTT, ARIZONA

6/3
98.3 FM

This place was packed daily a few years ago until a flood hit. It's also a fallout shelter and WPA project, so it has a somewhat disastrous reputation. "Everyone in town will pass through these doors," says the center director. Heaviest nontraumatic action: weekdays, noon to 2.

Phoenix *Don't bother checking out the action at Encanto Park until the shadows get long. (Herb Berwald)*

INDIAN SCHOOL PARK
HAYDEN AND CAMELBACK
SCOTTSDALE, ARIZONA

 4/2 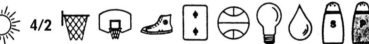   94.5 FM

A practice site for the San Francisco Giants every spring, this park has complete locker room and shower facilities. Say hey!

JACOBS PARK
FAIRVIEW AND LIND
TUCSON, ARIZONA

 6/3    93.7 FM

Tucson is loaded with parks, and the hooping here—just off the Miracle Mile strip—is as good as anywhere in town. Two rec centers, with gyms, are about to go up at Reid and Mo Udall parks. Mo Udall—now there's a pol who could J.

ARKANSAS

RALPH BUNCHE PARK
SOUTHEAST AND DIXIE
BENTON, ARKANSAS

103.7 FM

Perhaps in honor of the namesake for this spot, which sits "on the hill," there's a lot of Around-the-World played when a run can't be drummed up.

YOUTH CENTER AND BOYS CLUB
915 CALIFORNIA
FAYETTEVILLE, ARKANSAS

92.1 FM

The best off-campus spot in a hog-wild town. As you might expect from an academic grove, there's a lively noontime crowd. You can either join up, or pay a buck per visit.

EARL BELL COMMUNITY CENTER
1212 SOUTH CHURCH
JONESBORO, ARKANSAS

101.9 FM

Built in '36 as a WPA project, the center is named after the '84 Olympic bronze medalist in the pole vault. "We're not a rich town," says a local. "Other towns can give their heroes cars; all we can do is name a fifty-year-old building after him." They only play half over at Optimist Club Park, but there are four well-kept single hoops there.

MACARTHUR PARK
11TH AND MACALMONT
LITTLE ROCK, ARKANSAS

 2/1   1250 AM

Still one of Little Rock's best runs. The city provides no luminescence, but Sidney Moncrief has been known to light things up on occasion.

BILLY MITCHELL BOYS CLUB
3107 WEST 5TH
LITTLE ROCK, ARKANSAS

6/3   1250 AM

Sidney Moncrief played here, too (guy sure gets around). Still does, as a matter of fact, during the off-season.

BRYANT STREET PARK
BRYANT AND BULLARD
PINE BLUFF, ARKANSAS

 4/2      1340 AM

The regulars prefer half court here, where subversion, in the form of tennis, infiltrates and renders useless one slab from April 'til September.

IRON MOUNTAIN NEIGHBORHOOD CENTER
1101 CHURCH
TEXARKANA, ARKANSAS

 2/1      107.1 FM

The most active of eight courts around town. The summer league has folded, but fret not: a slam-dunk contest lights up the sky over the July 4th weekend.

THE KINGS OF KINGS

There are schoolyards named for Crispus Attucks, parks memorializing Frederick Douglass, rec centers honoring Booker T. Washington, playgrounds bearing the name of Ralph Bunche, and junior college gyms with "Malcolm X" chiseled on their cornerstones. But none of the aforementioned late greats comes close to challenging the Reverend Doctor Martin Luther King, Junior, whose mouthful of a moniker crops up at more parks, slabs, and rec centers than the most rodentlike gym rat. From Michigan to Illinois, upstate New York to Indiana, Minnesota to Texas—indeed, almost from the prodigious hilltops of New Hampshire to Lookout Mountain of Tennessee—you'll find the name of Dr. K gracing the proving grounds of tomorrow's Dr. Js.

So, which is best? For raw comp, we'll take Dallas's MLK Community Center, where a summer-league team boasting both Mark Aguirre and Rolando Blackman once finished *second*. For atmosphere, go with MLK Park in Grand Rapids, whose distinguishing feature is a King-style preacher. To see a thriving youth program, march on Washington, and the District's MLK Rec Center. And for keeping the spirit alive, nothing beats Buffalo's MLK Park, where summer-league officials are seriously considering building an enormous rainproof bubble over the court. They have a dream.

A creative maintenance man lent a regal flourish to center court at Dallas's Kingdome.

CALIFORNIA

CALIFORNIA PARK
OWENS AND CALIFORNIA
BAKERSFIELD, CALIFORNIA

8/4   107.9 FM

Teeming with activity. It doesn't rain much here, but when it does, undaunted regulars bring their boxes anyway, with tapes wrapped in plastic bags.

LIVE OAK PARK
SHATTUCK AND BERRYMAN
BERKELEY, CALIFORNIA

2/1   102.9 FM

For thirty years this spot has had maximal use, year-round. The primary game is three-on-three. A deeper tradition, which includes Bill Russell and attracts college recruiters, still thrives over at Grove Street Park, where a robust summer league exists.

RECREATIONAL SPORTS FACILITY
UNIVERSITY OF CALIFORNIA
BERKELEY, CALIFORNIA

14/7

                                                        1310 AM

You never have to wait for a run here, where the courts are as much in abundance as the comp. Being Berkeley, there's a great mix of people and personalities.

Century City *The Court of Law's many lawyers, asphalt and otherwise, make sure points of view get rendered dramatically. (Budd Symes)*

COURT OF LAW
11377 OLYMPIC
CENTURY CITY, CALIFORNIA

 2/1   **102.3 FM**

The law firm that built this secluded spot fields a legal-league power-house, so the comp occasionally gets respectable. Otherwise, the setting's the thing: beautiful landscaping, with a bistro bar and restaurant just steps away.

LENDERS PARK
1100 EAST ROSECRANS
COMPTON, CALIFORNIA

6/3   **1580 AM**

The game is of the run-and-gun, rise-and-shine variety, with attendant verbal byplay. You'll find a more taciturn run over at Wilson Park, where ladies come by to check out the scene.

NORTH GYM
FRESNO STATE UNIVERSITY
FRESNO, CALIFORNIA

12/6   95.7 FM

Off-season weekdays from 4 'til 7 are prime time here, where ex-Bull-dogs like Rod Higgins, Ron Anderson, and Bernard Thompson keep sharp during the summer.

POINSETTIA REC CENTER
POINSETTIA AND WILLOUGHBY
HOLLYWOOD, CALIFORNIA

 5/1   102.3 FM

Take a jumper, take a meeting—it's all in a day's work for the clientele here, where Hollywood's finest hang out. Look for actor Roger Moseby at the domino table.

ROGERS PARK
WEST BEACH AND EUCALYPTUS
INGLEWOOD, CALIFORNIA

2/1   102.3 FM

Games vary in roughness, depending on the hour and clientele. The rockfish reserve the gym. Michael Cooper has been known to show.

LAGUNA BEACH PLAYGROUND
PACIFIC COAST
LAGUNA BEACH, CALIFORNIA

 2/0   95.9 FM

Anyone accused of being unable to throw it in the ocean has the chance to demonstrate otherwise. The summer league is really a series of terrific weekend three-on-three tournaments. As ever, eight are required to play two-on-two at Laguna: four to run, and four more to share the experience.

In spite of the Topsiders, suburban ride, and apostate bumper sticker, Jeff LaPittus—here with homeboy Matt, who's modeling the fraternity look—gets special license.

A PRETTY DRIVING MOVE

Jeff LaPittus, a jones sufferer from Reseda, California, knew he had reached the age of majority when a girlfriend gave him this blue-plate special on his eighteenth birthday. Now, gas station attendants nod their heads knowingly when he pulls in his Datsun for a fill-up, and motorists mime challenges as they pass him on the San Diego Freeway. "It would *really* be fun on a car that was more ostentatious, like a Corvette or Ferrari," LaPittus says. "But it's a kick just the same." And it keeps tailgaters at bay.

THE BAY
OCEAN AND BAYSHORE
LONG BEACH, CALIFORNIA

 4/0      102.3 FM

Lots of three-on-three here, with participants cooled by the breezes off Los Alamitos Bay. Greet Basketball Sam, who'll hand you a business card with his motto, HAVE MOVES, WILL PLAY.

16

FIRESTONE FIELDHOUSE
PEPPERDINE UNIVERSITY
MALIBU, CALIFORNIA

4/2  **1580 FM**

The occasional pro, the occasional celeb, and the occasional water polo fish out of water. The evening and weekend action is best.

LIVE OAK PARK
18TH AND VALLEY
MANHATTAN BEACH, CALIFORNIA

 5/2  **102.3 FM**

Solid full-court runs here, but keep the language clean or the city will have the racks removed. It's happened before.

BUSHROD REC CENTER
59TH AND TELEGRAPH
OAKLAND, CALIFORNIA

2/1  **107.7 FM**

Spectators ring the court, taking in the games on the tile floor, while a couple of netless half courts sit outdoors. For more modern facilities, check out Rainbow Rec Center; for Oakland's liveliest outdoor scene, it's Mosswood Park, where there's a three-on-three tourney every July.

DEL REY LAGOON COURT
CONROY AND PACIFIC
PLAYA DEL RAY, CALIFORNIA

 3/1  **102.3 FM**

Just steps away from the beach, where the occasional MTV video is shot. Weekends, the action is nonstop. A great combo of beach ambience without the attendant sand patches that can make earnest hooping treacherous.

17

Playa del Rey *The Del Rey Lagoon is brackish; the play beside it rack-ish, with the pursuit of bounds usually less mellow than this. (Budd Symes)*

MCKINLEY PARK
ALHAMBRA AND F
SACRAMENTO, CALIFORNIA

 2/1   106.5 FM

Can you mount McKinley? Games run to twenty, win by two. Women don't play much, but watch. Perhaps that's why there's so much show-boating.

HERNANDEZ CENTER
222 NORTH LUGO
SAN BERNARDINO, CALIFORNIA

6/3   89.1 FM

This spot, named after the city employee who spearheaded the lobbying effort that got it built, has some Hispanic clientele, but bros do the principal hanging.

BALBOA PARK MUNICIPAL GYM
PAN AMERICAN AND PRESIDENTS
SAN DIEGO, CALIFORNIA

6/3      92.5 FM

Built for a city expo during the 30s, this has become San Diego's top spot. When it gets really busy, you play by the clock, not to a score. Open all day. Local TV stations make occasional forays here to get a word with the regulars. (It ought to be like a ski report: "Conditions good to excellent, runnin' 6'6" to 6'8". . . . .") Roughest games on the middle court.

NAVAL BASE GYM
SAN DIEGO NAVAL BASE
SAN DIEGO, CALIFORNIA

4/1   1360 AM

A decidedly inner-city atmosphere, with the maintenance of reps higher priority than simple winning. A house put together here may hold court for hours.

OCEAN BEACH REC CENTER
SANTA MONICA AND SUNSET CLIFF
SAN DIEGO, CALIFORNIA

 4/2    92.5 FM

A wonderful beach location that attracts a big afternoon crowd. Beware the water fountain, which is full of sand. Those who forgot their SPF 4 suntan lotion can repair to a couple of additional courts indoors.

MOSCONE PLAYGROUND
LAGUNA AND BAY
SAN FRANCISCO, CALIFORNIA

 2/1    100.9 FM

Formerly Funston Park, this spot has many pluses: the surface, the weather, the proximity to the bay, and easy access to BART (he's not a regular, but the subway that rumbles underfoot). When the fog rolls in, scoot indoors where there's another (short) court. More than they can do at Candlestick.

*Rec Center director Jon Greenberg
has discouraged antisocial behavior
on San Francisco's Potrero Hill by
making mugging acceptable.
(George Kruse)*

POTRERO HILL REC CENTER
22ND AND ARKANSAS
SAN FRANCISCO, CALIFORNIA

6/3    102.9 FM

While the Bay Area's best winter and summer league action rages indoors, those thirty and over take refuge on the outdoor slab. Be sure to play Ping-Pong at the table donated by the Dallas Mavericks, who work out here whenever they're in town.

WALL OF FAME

Should you find yourself barreling in for a slam at one basket in San Francisco's Potrero Hill Rec Center, watch out. You could be in for more face than you bargained for. Your momentum may take you flush with the gym's east wall, where the faces of some of the Bay Area's best players make up one of the most roguish of galleries. There's the smug mug of O. J. Simpson. The vicious visage of Quintin Dailey. The likenesses of Kurt Rambis, Wallace Bryant, Bernard King, and many of the less storied ballplayers who have honed their games at Potrero Hill.

It all started when center director Jon Greenberg, realizing that "these guys want some visibility, they want to be recognized," began putting index finger to Pentax shutter. Now Greenberg is going on his third decade as photographer and curator of The Wall, which has grown to three feet high and some forty feet long. He treats his portraits with the veneration that a Hoving would, using a clear plastic covering to shield them from errant lead passes. To a man, regulars at The Hill show reciprocal respect for The Wall and its hallowed hall. "It may be," says Greenberg, "one of the reasons we have no graffiti or vandalism here."

REC CENTER
MILL AND SANTA ROSA
SAN LUIS OBISPO, CALIFORNIA

 2/1   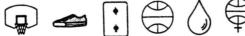   98 FM

If kids show, they get their own hoop, with adults banished to another. Pick-up play rages whenever there's no class in the gym here, which has been the place in SLO for more than forty years.

BO'S DRIVEWAY
2534 WEST HARVARD
SANTA ANA, CALIFORNIA

 1/0      95.9 FM

Lucille Bokosky knows what it's like to have a living room turned into a locker room and delicatessen at the same time. That's because her son Mike has made a habit of inviting his buddies over on the third Saturday of every August for a little ball. Of the 250-some-odd people who appear, only a select few get to play two-on-two, on teams picked out of two hats, one containing big guys' names, the other, little guys'. But the rest don't mind watching, and eating, and drinking, and kibbitzing. Way to go, Mrs. Bo.

ROBERTSON COURTS
UNIVERSITY OF CALIFORNIA
SANTA BARBARA, CALIFORNIA

 10/5      91.9 FM

Hot, tired, dripping with sweat—where do you go for aitch-two-oh? Your choice: the beach (a five-minute stroll) or the pool (not 200 yards away). "This place is very Santa Barbara," says a regular, "with no pressure to be the playmaker of the decade."

HOMESTEAD PARK
3445 BENTON
SANTA CLARA, CALIFORNIA

 4/2   105.7 FM

Smack in the middle of Silicon Valley. Alas, even the miracle of the microchip can't keep the lights burning past 11.

MEMORIAL PARK GYM
1401 OLYMPIC
SANTA MONICA, CALIFORNIA

8/4   1580 AM

Lakers and Clippers, 'SC and 'CLA—they all play. But so do the Pride 'n' Poise Boys, the Raiders. Adjust your playing style accordingly.

Venice Beach *With all the narcissistic vibes around, few dawdle before launching their J's at the Beach Courts. (Budd Symes)*

BEACH COURTS
OFF-THE-BOARDWALK
VENICE BEACH, CALIFORNIA

  4/2      102.3 FM

Physical culturalists abound at this spot, described by one person in the know as having ''too many chiefs and no Indians.'' Still, for raw atmosphere, the best in the West. Don't miss the annual California Championships staged by the New Social Workers each Memorial Day weekend. They offer women's—and men's—bathing suit contests between games.

REC CENTER
LINCOLN AND MANCHESTER
WESTCHESTER, CALIFORNIA

  2/1      102.3 FM

This is in suburban L.A., near the airport. Lights burn 'til 10:30 for pick-up; ballplayers 6' and under will want to check out the leagues reserved for them. Many wander over from nearby Loyola Marymount.

COLORADO

NORTH JEFFCO PARK
BROOKS AND CHASE
ARVADA, COLORADO

 2/1
1510 AM

High schoolers predominate, with best runs around dinnertime. Greater Denver's 'burbiest spot.

CANYON PARK
21ST AND CANYON
BOULDER, COLORADO

 2/1
97.3 FM

Few outdoor facilities are as fetching or as lively. Please don't park in the nearby apartment buildings' lots; that, as a stern sign warns, "may result in basketball court removal."

MEN'S GYM
UNIVERSITY OF COLORADO
BOULDER, COLORADO

6/3
97.3 FM

The biggest hazard here isn't so much the occasional Bronco or Buff gridder who shows, but the wall under each hoop that's considered the out-of-bounds marker. The sporting thing to do would be to concede breakaways—but don't count on it. No Docs play early Tuesday mornings—just post-docs.

Boulder *When the ball hits the peak of the backboard, as it's doing here at Canyon Park, it's in play. (Leslie Robinson)*

BOULDER PARK
BOULDER AND HANCOCK
COLORADO SPRINGS, COLORADO

 2/1      90.5 FM

Go west of this spot, young man—to Memorial Hospital, should you get hurt, and to the Olympic Training Center, should you have higher aspirations.

PIKES PEAK YMCA/USO
207 NORTH NEVADA
COLORADO SPRINGS, COLORADO

8/4      90.5 FM

Noontime games—11:30 'til 1:30, to be precise—aren't for claustrophobes: they're run five-on-five half court, and hew to a strict set of posted rules.

11TH STREET PARK
11TH AND SYRACUSE
DENVER, COLORADO

 2/1      1510 AM

The Rockies form a picturesque backdrop to the runs here, which are generally civil. Less so is the surface, an uneven blacktop that has done in more than its share of ankles.

RED SHIELD CORPS COMMUNITY CENTER
29TH AND HIGH
DENVER, COLORADO

6/3      1510 AM

Site of Denver's NBA Pro-Am, in addition to a lively summer league for the more mortal. Usually two full-court games go on simultaneously; sometimes, mostly in May before the summer league starts, games are limited to fifteen minutes or twelve points. A full court outdoors, too. Glen Arm Rec Center is one sneaker-style down in comp, but definitely worth a look.

20TH STREET GYM
20TH AND CURTIS
DENVER, COLORADO

2/1   1510 AM

Red Shield may have the leagues, but this spot is the Mile High City's original pick-up spot. The close quarters mean: (1) full court is played almost exclusively; and (2) the gym reaches 115 degrees on some Godforsaken days. Just steps from the bus station; try roping a few transients into a run.

Denver Many passing through the portals at 20th Street have had checkered careers.

INTRAMURAL GYM
COLORADO STATE UNIVERSITY
FORT COLLINS, COLORADO

6/3   **93.3 FM**

There's a slab of outdoor courts nearby, but the serious action takes place here, indoors. Spring and fall are the best times to go.

GLENDALE PARK
CHERRY AND TENNESSEE
GLENDALE, COLORADO

 6/3   **1510 AM**

The spot for al fresco hoop on Denver's East Side. The crowd gathers late in the day, so thank goodness for the lights.

BITTERSWEET PARK
35TH AND SIXTEENTH
GREELEY, COLORADO

 2/1   **1310 AM**

A huge park with lots of diversions. Be kind to all the joggers. You may want to check out the slightly more collegiate crowds over at Farr Park and Northern Colorado's Gunter Hall.

INTERMEDIATE SCHOOL REC COMPLEX
WEST 6TH AND MCWETHY
LEADVILLE, COLORADO

4/2   **1230 AM**

Is this as high as you'll ever get? At an elevation of 10,125, a full-court run could leave you feeling on top of the world—and a little short of breath.

CONNECTICUT

TOMLINSON JUNIOR HIGH SCHOOLYARD
200 UNQUOWA
FAIRFIELD, CONNECTICUT

 2/1   600 AM

Be prepared for plenty of touchy-feely stuff under the rack, and don't call any cheap fouls. A first-rate summer spot, with best runs on Wednesday evenings and weekend mornings.

WASHINGTON PARK
MITCHELL AND MERIDIAN
GROTON, CONNECTICUT

 4/2   105.5 FM

The show doesn't go on without a full-court quorum here, where five-on-five is the main event. Weekday evenings are the best times to rock.

ELIZABETH PARK
ELIZABETH AND WHITNEY
HARTFORD, CONNECTICUT

 4/2   96.5 FM

People play here constantly during the summer; winter, too, when the weather breaks. Older guys aren't as physical as the young'uns, who, according to one insider, "gotta prove themselves." Also check out Keney Park, more of a neighborhood spot, but occasionally Elizabeth's equal.

YMCA CENTRAL BRANCH
JEWELL AND PEARL
HARTFORD, CONNECTICUT

6/3   96.5 FM

This being the actuarial capital of the world, guys keep good track of the score. Watch out for the fellow in the AETNA, WE'RE GLAD WE MET YA *T-shirt.*

SURF CLUB
SURF CLUB COURT
MADISON, CONNECTICUT

 4/2      94.3 FM

Everybody runs ''skins'' at this beachside spot, where an Independence Day tournament ends with fireworks and a party. The place rocks on weekend mornings around 9, when collegians past and present show.

WASHINGTON PARK
WASHINGTON
NEW BRITAIN, CONNECTICUT

 4/2      96.5 FM

The spot that spawned Rod (Rocket) Foster now boasts Mel (Magic) Kline and Tony (Apache) Gonzalez, and a summer league replete with a three-point line. Rich white kids, beware: Al, the league director, steams when you bolt your team midseason to attend hoop camp.

GOFF STREET PLAYGROUND
GOFF AND SHERMAN
NEW HAVEN, CONNECTICUT

 4/2      94.3 FM

Be sure yo' game is in order before showing yo' face at Goff Street. Mere spectators, of course, are welcome, too—and will likely be rewarded with an appearance by Sly Williams, John Williamson, or Calvin Murphy, who sometimes spins his baton for the multitudes.

29

New Haven *At Goff Street a defender is about to join the net in the ranks of the used. (Rollin Riggs)*

PAYNE WHITNEY GYM
YALE UNIVERSITY
NEW HAVEN, CONNECTICUT

4/2   **94.3 FM**

Something with fourteen floors that goes by the name ''Payne Whitney'' sounds more like a brokerage house. Indeed, security keeps it exclusive, making it difficult for non-Yalies to run. Good luck sneaking in.

SCALZI PARK
BRIDGE AND WASHINGTON
STAMFORD, CONNECTICUT

 2/1   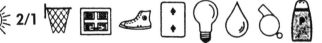 **96.7 FM**

You may find Connecticut honkeys on King Arthur's Court, but not on this one. The scene is more interracial at the Monday-night concerts during the summer—and on the bocce courts.

30

SIMSBURY FARMS REC COMPLEX
100 OLD FARMS
SIMSBURY, CONNECTICUT

 4/2   96.5 FM

This spot falls under the aegis of Gerry, the local rec director (see ''The Suburban Look,'' The In-Your-Face Basketball Book*), and his well-bred expression of confidence. The pond just off the court's north end supplies a nice exurban touch—but will claim the errant pass or air ball.*

Waterbury *Pearl Street fashion plate Darryl Dawkins models his community-center chest. Says Hubie, P.S.C.C. hoops maven, ''People have been* mugged *for a shirt like that.'' Not, presumably, the Dawk. (Don Cousey)*

PEARL STREET COMMUNITY CENTER
PEARL
WATERBURY, CONNECTICUT

 4/2   1240 AM

A sweet name for a sweet spot that draws collegians (Fairfield, UConn, Central Connecticut State) and pros (Wes Matthews and John Bagley).

WOLCOTT PARK
NEW BRITAIN
WEST HARTFORD, CONNECTICUT

 4/2   96.5 FM

This is a ritzy, wealthy 'burb, so play here tends to be of the Caucasian persuasion.

31

DELAWARE

DISCIPLES OF CHRIST COURT
PENNSYLVANIA AND GARFIELD
BETHANY BEACH, DELAWARE

 2/1   95.9 FM

The slimmest lanes you'll ever see. The nearby Christian Conference Center, which is run by the Disciples of Christ, has been known to pass the hat among hoopsters who use the court.

DOVER STREET PARK
NEW AND DOVER
DOVER, DELAWARE

 2/1   1410 AM

Brothers from another neighborhood court—at Kirkwood and Division—will cruise by, ready to rock the Dover Street regulars.

CARPENTER SPORTS BUILDING
UNIVERSITY OF DELAWARE
NEWARK, DELAWARE

12/6   91.3 FM

Only Blue Hen students are permitted here. Sneaking in is tough, though a few townies have turned the trick. When the weather is nice, much of the action gravitates outdoors to the Rodney Dormitory courts, where no one checks IDs.

BONSALL PARK
SILVERSIDE AND FAULK
WILMINGTON, DELAWARE

  4/2   93.7 FM

Bonsall has those long, natural-fiber nets hanging from the racks. Swish a high-arching J with plenty of backspin, and you'll hear what sounds like a slap on the ass.

WEST CENTER CITY COMMUNITY CENTER
MADISON AND 6TH
WILMINGTON, DELAWARE

 6/3   93.7 FM

In the summer the gym is AC cool and the hoop blast-furnace hot, thanks largely to an NCAA-sanctioned loop that bans all zone defenses. Winter pick-up is played with a fifteen-minute running clock, but you don't play unless you sign up with Arnold.

FLORIDA

SAN LANDO PARK
401 WEST HIGHLAND
ALTAMONTE SPRINGS, FLORIDA

 4/2

This place, a haven for hackers, screamers, debaters, and head cases, is utter and total confusion. Bodies by Fisher; minds by Mattel.

INTRAMURAL COURTS
UNIVERSITY OF MIAMI
CORAL GABLES, FLORIDA

 12/6

At Suntan U., almost anything goes; they do, unfortunately, check for IDs. This has such potential to be a mecca that school officials take all the rims down over breaks—about what you'd expect from a college that abolished hoop for fourteen years.

SEABREEZE REC CENTER
ATLANTIC
DAYTONA BEACH, FLORIDA

 2/1

Just because your opponent is wearing sandals doesn't mean he takes you for a chump; it's the standard here. The comp can vary drastically, depending on who's blowing through town.

HOLIDAY PARK GYM
1101 HOLIDAY PARK
FT. LAUDERDALE, FLORIDA

8/4   **1490 AM**

Where the boys are, at least over Memorial Day weekend, when an annual tournament attracts some of the state's best streetballers.

SOUTH BEACH COURTS
SOUTH ATLANTIC (AIA)
FORT LAUDERDALE, FLORIDA

 4/2    **103 FM**

Slippery when sandy, which is to say all the time. Right on the beach, within staggering distance of The Button, The Ocean Mist, and other such shrines. Spring-break action is like the Olympics: clashes of cultures and styles—everything but the singing of anthems.

Fort Lauderdale *At the South Beach Courts the fastbreak action is a spring break ritual, and a palm isn't a violation. (Florida FotoBanc)*

FLORIDA GYM
UNIVERSITY OF FLORIDA
GAINESVILLE, FLORIDA

6/3
105.5 FM

The doors don't get shut 'til 11:30 P.M., so you can squeeze in your hooping as needed. The main run is on the north court.

JEFFERSON PLAYGROUND
JEFFERSON
JACKSONVILLE, FLORIDA

 12/2
1400 AM

Kids' Annex:

 6/2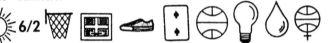

The most racks in Jax. Holly's Bar-B-Q still makes the rounds, doing big business, especially at the Kids' Annex.

SIMON JOHNSON COMMUNITY CENTER
ROYAL AND MONCRIEF
JACKSONVILLE, FLORIDA

 4/1
1400 AM

Though Truck Robinson played here when he was nothing but a Tonka Toy, the locals are quite content with an address on Moncrief. Runs gear up late afternoons.

ARCHER JUNIOR HIGH SCHOOLYARD
WHITE AND UNITED
KEY WEST, FLORIDA

 4/2
92.5 FM

Cuban refugees are among the clientele here, where games begin early on weekends. If access can be secured, the school gym—despite its floor, soft from extensive termite damage—is preferred.

RON EHMANN PARK
10995 SOUTHWEST 97TH
MIAMI, FLORIDA

 4/2    95 FM

"It's hidden by trees, and that keeps the hackers away," says Cesar Odio, one of this city's premier Cuban-American pick-up players. Cagey games, with few arguments. Particularly popular during Daylight Savings Time, because there are no lights.

TAMIAMI REGIONAL PARK
24TH AND NINETEENTH
MIAMI, FLORIDA

 2/1   99.1 FM

One of south Florida's most physical and forensic facilities. Anyone caught in a sandwich pick here knows the meaning of Miami vise.

TROPICAL PARK
7900 SOUTHWEST 40TH
MIAMI, FLORIDA

 4/2    108 FM

The melting pot smolders at this converted racetrack, in intense and sometimes acrimonious games. Boxer Alexis Arguello occasionally spars in the nearby ring; don't be surprised to find fisticuffs extending to the wood, too. We've recommended a salsa station, and advise your uttering "en tu cara"—that's Spanish for "in your face"—with discretion.

PUBLIC COURT
PALM ISLAND
MIAMI BEACH, FLORIDA

 2/1    99.1 FM

There's a guard gate, and the rent-a-cop'll write down your license-plate number. But don't let him give you a hard time, for this is a public park. A beaut of a spot in the middle of Biscayne Bay, always a

Miami Beach *The* Heralded *Palm Island court, just off the causeway, is a sublime slab in search of a game.*

few degrees cooler than Miami proper. Named south Florida's finest hoops court by The Miami Herald—*and we thought we were the only people who kept track of such things.*

COMMUNITY CENTER
1200 PROSPERITY FARMS
NORTH PALM BEACH, FLORIDA

6/3      98.6 FM

Noteworthy if for no other reason than it's the site of the Florida Parks & Rec Department's statewide slam-dunk championships. Talk about a state of excitement . . .

LORNA DOONE PARK
CHURCH AND RIO GRANDE
ORLANDO, FLORIDA

 2/1    1270 AM

Unwary suburbanites can expect to be chewed up and devoured like sugar cookies.

38

COMMUNITY CENTER
4404 BURNS
PALM BEACH GARDENS, FLORIDA

4/2   98.6 FM

The gym's available for plenty of free play, and Tom, the super, even throws the doors open at some clandestine times for regulars. Get on his good side and you'll be able to run with the vets.

MORRIS COURT
CORD AND J
PENSACOLA, FLORIDA

 4/2   980 AM

The In-Your-Face *address award. If some Pensacolan says, ''Take J 'til you hit Cord,'' you've gotten directions* and *advice.*

SPORTSMEN'S PARK
295 N.W. PRIMA VISTA
PORT ST. LUCIE, FLORIDA

 4/1      1400 AM

The comp isn't much to shout about, though there's plenty of shouting supplied by *the comp. If you want to avoid setting some of it off, don't call a charge.*

HURLEY PARK
GULF AND 15TH
ST. PETERSBURG BEACH, FLORIDA

 2/1    104.7 FM

Services a regular weekend clientele, which frequently adjourns to one of the many nearby bars.

Sanford *You'll find plenty of junk launched hoopward when Sanford's sons show at the Civic Center court. (Brian LaPeter)*

SANFORD CIVIC CENTER
401 EAST SEMINOLE
SANFORD, FLORIDA

 2/1   1400 AM

Kiddie heaven on earth. The rims top out at 8½', and the court is loaded with Biddy Ballers during the day. Five-teners come by to Bol-ly the Lilliputians.

DADE STREET COMMUNITY CENTER
1115 NORTH DADE
TALLAHASSEE, FLORIDA

2/1   **104.1 FM**

The summer league here is the highlight of the local rec-hall-ball season.

RIVERFRONT PARK
1000 NORTH BOULEVARD
TAMPA, FLORIDA

 5/2      **104.7 FM**

On a sunny Sunday there's no finer place to be in all of Tampa. You can chill out, if not exactly keep cool. The summer league is top-drawer.

AZALEA LANE REC CENTER
MINNESOTA AND AZALEA
WINTER PARK, FLORIDA

 6/3      **1270 AM**

With no painted boundary lines to go by, you get your bearings from cracks in the pavement. Among high schoolers, the quality of play is exceptionally high.

GEORGIA

MAPLE STREET COURT
MAPLE
ALBANY, GEORGIA

 2/1   96.3 FM

An O.K. place to play, though better runs are to be found at the Thorn-ton Community Center, and among juniors at the Y or the Jefferson Street Boys Club. Crank out the juice on 96.3, a.k.a. Total Control.

CHASTAIN PARK
NORTH SIDE AND WIEUCA WEST
ATLANTA, GEORGIA

6/3   96.1 FM

The rubberized floor gives you more bounce to the ounce. Ask about the legendary Fish, who always insists on running skins, the better to show off a nasty scar. Best runs noonish, early in the week.

DOWNTOWN ATHLETIC CLUB
OMNI INTERNATIONAL HOTEL
ATLANTA, GEORGIA

2/1   96.1 FM

You can do everything except order rebounds from room service at this spot, a full court in a racquetball court in a ritzy downtown hotel. Challenge a bellhop to a run.

GRANT PARK
537 PARK S.W.
ATLANTA, GEORGIA

 4/2   96.1 FM

Three-on-three is big here, with best comp showing up on weekday evenings and Sunday afternoons. A gym next door has a beautiful floor and more serious ballplayers.

RALPH MCGILL PLAYGROUND
RALPH MCGILL
ATLANTA, GEORGIA

 4/2   96.1 FM

A serviceable court, but somewhat disappointing for the South's hub city. One local puts the Atlanta scene in perspective: "The outdoor courts aren't well maintained, and indoor spots are too expensive. A lot of the clubs, including the Ys, are locked into the Racquetball Syndrome. It's a shame. The outdoor game could be great here."

EISENHOWER-ARMY MED CENTER COURT
FORT GORDON
AUGUSTA, GEORGIA

2/1 103 FM

Entertain the patients, who watch the action from their beds, and don't let the air currents from the occasional chopper affect your jumper.

WARREN ROAD COMMUNITY CENTER
300 WARREN
AUGUSTA, GEORGIA

 6/3   103 FM

As one regular puts it, "There's more to Augusta than golf and the Masters." Most of the city's serious players do their running at "The Road."

43

REGGIE'S COURT

The road from Waycross to Savannah isn't a particularly pretty one. Long stretches of red Georgia clay are studded with hardscrabble small towns. But there is something of an oasis along the way—an oasis of the spirit, at least. Shoehorned in between a roadside tavern, a pool hall, and a dilapidated soul-food restaurant is a bleached slab of concrete with two fine-looking half-moons at either end. Accurate markings have been painted on the cement, and string nets laced lovingly to the rims.

"Whose is it?" you ask the barkeep.

"Reggie's court," he burps back.

"Reggie?"

"Yeah. Lives with his mama in that house next to it."

"He there now?"

"Nope. Probably at work."

Questions linger about Reggie, but they aren't asked. It's probably best to leave the details of his inspiration to the imagination. Just the same, it would be great to see someone from Richmond Hill, Georgia, make it big.

Soul food and string music are equally sweet in Richmond Hill, where thanks to Reggie you don't have to play on red clay.

3RD AVENUE PARK
3RD AND VINE
DAWSON, GEORGIA

 2/1    990 AM

Third and Vine is a long way from Hollywood and Vine, but just a block away from the downtown stores and hangouts.

HILLCREST PARK
HILLCREST
MACON, GEORGIA

 6/3      1240 AM

Macon's been makin' stars out of quite a few guys over the years—Elmore Smith, Norm Nixon, and Jeff Malone, to name several. This town almost did the same for little Walter Daniels, who went from being a plumber to getting to drain Js for the Spurs in the preseason a while back. Like snowbirds, the play heads south with winter, to Memorial Park's gym.

LAWRENCE REC CENTER
LAWRENCE
MARIETTA, GEORGIA

 6/3   103.3 FM

Unquestionably metro Atlanta's best run, as Dale Ellis and Cedric Henderson can attest. The Elizabeth Porter Rec Center over on Montgomery also gets high marks.

TOWN PARK
BUTTS MILLS
PINE MOUNTAIN, GEORGIA

 4/1    1340 AM

The main full-slab is concrete; two warm-up hoops are on dirt. Team-oriented ball prevails, from 6 'til dark—and surely would last longer if the authorities heeded regulars' pleas to have the lights fixed.

MAPLE STREET PARK GYM
MAPLE
ROME, GEORGIA

4/1  97.7 FM

One of three municipal gyms run by the county rec department. A lively drop-in clientele. Cramped quarters, so they run transcon here.

BLACKSHEAR COMPLEX
WHEATON AND HARMON
SAVANNAH, GEORGIA

12/6  93.1 FM

Savannah's number-1 outdoor spot specializes in hoops only: no tennis, no swimming, no pinochle, or other lame diversions. The supervisor, who's on duty from 9 'til 9, makes sure of it.

Savannah *You'd better be in shape if you show at Tompkins, where they play international rules to maximize the run. (Stephen T. Frazier)*

TOMPKINS REC CENTER
2323 OGEECEE
SAVANNAH, GEORGIA

93.3 FM

Games to twelve points or ten minutes, whichever comes first. A sink in an adjacent room serves as a drinking fountain. International inbounds rule—don't bother checking the ball on a change of possession—keeps the tempo up and everyone in shape.

WELLS PARK
39TH AND MONTGOMERY
SAVANNAH, GEORGIA

93.1 FM

All the trappings of urban life are around: car wash, minimart, serious hangers-out. Hoop hysteria is so acute here that all you have to do is show with pill, loft a few hoopward, and a game will materialize.

HAWAII

PAKI PLAYGROUND
PAKI AND KAPAHULU
HONOLULU, HAWAII

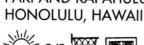   

Right next to the fire station, just steps from Waikiki beach. Roger Moseby (didn't we see him in Hollywood?) of Magnum, P.I. *fame sponsors a summer league team, and a soda machine provides refreshments. Got some negative pub in* Sports Illustrated *for the selfish style that prevails.*

WAILUKU GYM
MARKET
MAUI, HAWAII

Lots of leagues, but the comp is as calm as a tropical breeze. For outdoor hoop, check out Kalama Park in Kihei, or any schoolyard that happens to be hoppin'.

PUPUKEA BEACH PARK
KAMEHAMENA
OAHU, HAWAII

Best outdoor spot on the North Shore. It's not uncommon to find a surfer or two tapering off with a gnarly run or two, trying for max air.

48

SUNSET BEACH ELEMENTARY SCHOOLYARD
KAMEHAMENA
OAHU, HAWAII

 4/2   92.3 FM

Right across the street from the heart of the Banzai Pipeline, one of the world's most notorious surfing spots. If you're after shade, check out Swanzy Beach Park for a little, and the BYU-Hawaii gym for a lot.

Honolulu *It's every man for himself at Paki Playground, where the fire hoses are ready to cool off hot heads. (Wan Man To)*

IDAHO

YMCA
1530 WEST STATE
BOISE, IDAHO

2/1   92.3 FM

Here's one spot in the Land of the Spud that doesn't gather any cobwebs.

CITY PARK
MULLAN AND NORTHWEST
COEUR D'ALENE, IDAHO

 6/0   103.1 FM

These racks are on the lake, with the expected beachside sideshows—Idaho-style—in abundance. You can avoid getting French fried by cruising the gym at North Idaho College.

REC CENTER
520 MEMORIAL
IDAHO FALLS, IDAHO

6/3   1260 AM

The only place to play in town. The Falls's best leagues are fall leagues, which run from adult, to junior, to 6'-and-under.

50

AIRPORT PARK
6TH AND CEDAR
LEWISTON, IDAHO

 2/1
1350 AM

This spot's name conjures up an image of takeoffs and landings. Alas, the clientele is still awaiting FAA approval. The lights, from adjacent tennis courts, are adequate.

NBA BACKYARD ARENA
1741 SYRINGA
POCATELLO, IDAHO

 1/0
1290 AM

The Syringa Street Gang, a.k.a. the Neighborhood Basketball Association, gathers here annually for a round-robin one-on-one tournament. If you can survive the rough play, arguments, and three-point rule, you may get to cut down the net.

COLLEGE GYM
COLLEGE OF SOUTHERN IDAHO
TWIN FALLS, IDAHO

6/3
102.9 FM

Check out what it's like playing with the Snake River Canyon as your baseline. May your leaps end more artistically than Evel Knievel's.

WALTER JOHNSON MEMORIAL PARK
EAST 3RD AND GRAY
WEISER, IDAHO

 2/1
1260 AM

A refurbishing resulted in lines finally being painted. Still, as you might expect, ball and bat carry more import at this park, named after a Hall of Famer.

51

ILLINOIS

MCCULLOUGH PARK
150 WEST ILLINOIS
AURORA, ILLINOIS

6/3  107.9 FM

The breeding ground for many on the roster of a local AAU power-house. NBA journeyman Mickey Johnson may tote the biggest rep.

PYRAMID COURTS
CEDAR AND 13TH
CAIRO, ILLINOIS

 3/1  1490 AM

In a sense, first cuts at Cairo High take place in the vigorous pick-up games here. John Wooden may not agree, but kids in these parts see it as a Pyramid of success.

INTRAMURAL-REC BUILDING
SOUTHERN ILLINOIS UNIVERSITY
CARBONDALE, ILLINOIS

8/4 101.5 FM

Pick-up action rages all day. Unlike so many rec gyms with their new-fangled composition surfaces, the wood here is pure maple.

LEONHARD CENTER
2112 WEST SANGAMON
CHAMPAIGN, ILLINOIS

6/3    **94.5 FM**

An official Olivia Newton-John–sanctioned facility, with lots of getting physical by players who spend lots of time in the adjoining weight room. To keep the bumping and grinding in check, run-and-gun prevails.

CHITOWN

A dream tour of Chicago begins by hailing a taxicab. At the wheel is local hack Nat (Sweetwater) Clifton, the former Globetrotter and Knick, who knows exactly where to go. First, a Y for a noontime run. Then, the beach parks along the lake—Foster or Farwell—for some twilight action, from which you cool down with a long draw at a "bubbler," one of those ever-running drinking fountains that are commonplace here. After dusk falls, you tool by one of the many rec centers run by the Chicago Park District. Odds are you've had a memorable run at one of your three stops, for without this city's mother lode of talent, the Big Ten couldn't exist.

FARWELL BEACH COURT
FARWELL
CHICAGO, ILLINOIS

 1/0    **102.7 FM**

The location may be beachside, but the atmosphere is strictly urban. Sidney Green comes by for a little exercise once in a while, scaring off most of the hackers.

FOSTER BEACH COURT
FOSTER
CHICAGO, ILLINOIS

 2/1    **102.7 FM**

This spot draws 'em from all over the Chicagoland area on summer weekends, when the action is nonstop. A concession stand sits adjacent to the court.

Chicago *Up a few West Side stories, above the Marillac House Court, you can line up your three-pointers with the Sears Tower. (Geoffrey Biddle/Archive)*

MARILLAC HOUSE COURT
JACKSON AND CALIFORNIA
CHICAGO, ILLINOIS

 3/1   102.7 FM

A Catholic youth home, with leagues galore in the summer, and pick-up, says Jerry the super, "when time permits." As soon as the lights go out at 10, the court turns into a social center for this West Side neighborhood. Sister Yvonne makes sure no one practices bad habits.

NEW CITY YMCA
1515 NORTH HALSTEAD
CHICAGO, ILLINOIS

6/3    102.7 FM

A fairly new facility that's attracting many of Chicago's better players. They run weekdays, 11 to 2; Sunday morning services start at 9. Maurice Cheeks likes to break a summer sweat here, though on Saturdays everyone—Mo too—runs at the Lawson Y.

STUDENT REC CENTER
NORTHERN ILLINOIS UNIVERSITY
DEKALB, ILLINOIS

24/12   92.5 FM

With twenty-four hoops, you'd think this place would raise quite a din. Fact is, with its carpetlike surface, it may be the quietest indoor spot in the country.

BOYS CLUB
823 SUMMIT
EAST ST. LOUIS, ILLINOIS

 2/1   1490 AM

The rule here is simple: if the temp's 50 or above, there'll be a run. A relatively new court, with a rep that's still growing.

FRATERNITY COURTS
NORTHWESTERN UNIVERSITY
EVANSTON, ILLINOIS

 4/2   102.7 FM

The beach is a short stroll away, as are the kegs in the surrounding frat houses. Look for more serious action in nearby Patten Gym.

Franklin Park *The lady's making a fashion statement: the girls here get after the game head first. (Carl Wagner)*

FRANKLIN PARK PARK DISTRICT
9560 FRANKLIN
FRANKLIN PARK, ILLINOIS

This spot is home to the Chicagoland's number-1 women's league, but the guys are well represented, too, by a coterie of ex-DePaul studfish.

COOPER CENTER
150TH AND COOPER
HARVEY, ILLINOIS

The place in Harvey, frequented by such mid-level-pro and ex-pro rockers as Craig Hodges and Rod Higgins, as well as sundry collegians and streetballers.

DESPLAINES BASKETBALL COURTS
SOUTH MCDONOUGH
JOLIET, ILLINOIS

Breakdancers provide a regular sideshow, and an evening slam-dunk contest caps off each day's action.

WILKINS HALL COURTS
ILLINOIS STATE UNIVERSITY
NORMAL, ILLINOIS

The comp's not great. ''We're out here 'cause they're in there,'' says one undergrad, with a side glance at nearby Horton Field House, where the varsity types hang. These metal nets—they look like hula skirts designed for Grace Jones—are right next to a sandbox where they play ersatz beach volleyball. (You think that's something, check out nearby Fairview Park, where they've got a waterslide next to the courts.) Indoor runs? Try McCormick Hall, on campus.

BARRIE REC CENTER
LOMBARD AND GARFIELD
OAK PARK, ILLINOIS

  2/0

102.7 FM

Just a few blocks from Chitown proper, the West Side, to be precise. Not only are there no nets, but rim heights vary from week to week, depending on the extent of slam-jamming that's gone on.

Normal *At Illinois State's Wilkins Hall courts you leap next to a tall building for every single bound.*

PROCTOR REC CENTER
309 SOUTH ALLEN
PEORIA, ILLINOIS

 6/2
98.3 FM

Can you play in Peoria? Test yourself against the comp, including many Bradley players, who come 'round.

KEN-ROCK COMMUNITY CENTER
3218 11TH
ROCKFORD, ILLINOIS

2/1
97.5 FM

Neither parks nor hoops is high among officialdom's priorities, but this town still turns out its share of players. They, in turn, turn up here, usually late weekday afternoons.

REC CENTER
800 WEST ROMEO
ROMEOVILLE, ILLINOIS

6/3

Blue-collar players abound in this Chitown 'burb. Open seven days a week.

LANTHIER PARK
CONVERSE AND MICHIGAN
SPRINGFIELD, ILLINOIS

 4/2
98.7 FM

On Tuesday and Wednesday evenings, all games go to fifteen by ones. Of course, they're volleyball games, so plan on running every night of the week but. *On those two odd nights, try checking out the South 4th Street Y.*

INDIANA

HOOPSIERS

Is it any surprise that the first basketball game ever played outside the State of Massachusetts took place on a court above a tavern in Crawfordsville, Indiana? The small towns and 'burbs of this obsessed state produce all those Complete Players with their guile and unerring Js. It's the big cities, however—Indy and Gary—that could easily be Chicago, if you were to judge by quality of hoop alone. You'll find a smattering of make it, take it around the state, but for the most part Hoosiers would just as soon bear down and D up after scoring a bucket. At the same time, conflicting folkways are tolerated. As one hoopster in Franklin told us, with a shrug, "People play different, just like poker."

GEATER CENTER
CHASE AND 15TH
ANDERSON, INDIANA

 6/3  105.7 FM

There are few geeks at Geater, where Bobby Wilkerson, Ray Tolbert, and even Artis Gilmore have wheeled by.

HPER BUILDING
INDIANA UNIVERSITY
BLOOMINGTON, INDIANA

26/13  97 FM

With thirteen full slabs, you'd think getting a run would be easy. But during prime time, would-be challengers are lined up three-deep by each court, on painted numbers to indicate their priority. A three-ring circus of not-so-hurryin' Hoosiers.

59

LINCOLN PARK
25TH AND LINCOLN PARK
COLUMBUS, INDIANA

 2/1

Not the best court in town, but its constant activity makes it the place to be. You'll also find PT over at the Columbus East High Schoolyard (where they also run a summer league).

SUNNYSIDE PARK
141ST AND GRACE
EAST CHICAGO, INDIANA

 6/3

No hicks from French Lick, or other pedantic palefaces squaring up for textbook jumpers. Play is decidedly brotherly.

Evansville *When you're shooting at sewers, like the loose goals at Igleheart Park, you're more likely to drain the downtown J.*

IGLEHEART PARK
1ST AND STONEBRIDGE
EVANSVILLE, INDIANA

 2/1   1330 AM

The comp here has fallen off some since a few of the lights went out, but this is still the best outdoor run in a hoop-hysterical town. Like the tails of atomic dogs, the backboards wag to your jams.

RESERVOIR PARK
LAFAYETTE AND CLINTON
FORT WAYNE, INDIANA

 2/1      95.1 FM

Post B-ball, pool your talents and shoot a little 8-ball. In the Rez, as this park is known, you can turn the tables at the Cooper Community Center, on site.

COMMUNITY PARK
EAST KING AND YOUNG
FRANKLIN, INDIANA

 2/1      95.5 FM

Plenty of good play at this new spot, whose christening was postponed when workmen (obviously out-of-staters) installed hoops at 9'6". Indoor runs are found in the gym at the adjacent Wonder Five Center, named after a quality quintet of the '20s. And the friendliest game takes place at Province Park, where the folks in the brown house next to the court leave a pitcher and cups out for parched throats.

BRUNSWICK NEIGHBORHOOD CENTER
775 CLARK
GARY, INDIANA

2/1   107.5 FM

Always a good-size crowd, because this is one of the few indoor spots in town open to anyone.

61

BEN DAVIS HIGH SCHOOLYARD
10TH AND GIRLS SCHOOL
INDIANAPOLIS, INDIANA

 10/5   95 FM

Full-serve or self-serve, players of all octane ratings can find a run to match their skills here. The lights blaze into the night, and the juice isn't being wasted. For après *hoop, we stand by our recommendation of the Ponderosa out on the main drag, where you can get unlimited free refills on soft drinks.*

DOUGLASS PARK
25TH AND MARTINDALE
INDIANAPOLIS, INDIANA

 2/1   105.7 FM

The place on the East Side, which is noted for its physical style of play. A week-long Black Expo is held here every summer, complete with a thirty-two-team invitational tournament. The indoor court nearby extends the season year-round.

TARKINGTON PARK
38TH AND SHERIDAN
INDIANAPOLIS, INDIANA

 4/2   105.7 FM

There's a small shopping center nearby, so watch out when someone threatens to "take you to the cleaners."

FOSTER PARK
721 WEST SUPERIOR
KOKOMO, INDIANA

 4/2   93 FM

Not to be confused with Brooklyn's park of the same name. Kokomo fosters just as much hoicely passion.

MEMORIAL PARK
LEBANON AND CAMP
LEBANON, INDIANA

 2/1      100.9 FM

July 4 is tourney time in Lebanon, home of supershooter Rick Mount and now his son Richie. The city fathers, cross at hangers-out who hung on the rims at an adjacent court, are of no mind to put up new baskets there. Better treat these racks with respect.

CHARLES MILL DAM PARK
NORTH WASHINGTON
MARION, INDIANA

 2/1   95 FM

A great setting, right by the river. Dam right they can play at this swish spot, where loads of top-shelf schoolboys have played.

CITY PARK
HOME AND MORGAN
MARTINSVILLE, INDIANA

 6/3      1540 AM

The main homeboy is John Wooden, so see if you can't make like The Man and hold court for a dynastic run of runs.

McCULLOCH PARK
BROADWAY AND HIGHLAND
MUNCIE, INDIANA

 4/2      104.1 FM

There's good news and there's bad news. First, the good news: lights are being planned for the near future. The bad news: they'll be hitched to a timer on a strict 6 to 11 schedule.

63

Martinsville *They start picking up the rock early at City Park, and don't stop playing just because it gets dark. (Geoffrey Biddle/Archive)*

BAKER PARK
2100 SOUTH MAIN
NEW CASTLE, INDIANA

 4/2   93 FM

With such locals as Kent Benson and Steve Alford playing here, watch out or you'll get Knight-schooled.

CLEAR CREEK PARK
ROUTE 40 AND S.W. 11TH
RICHMOND, INDIANA

 6/3   101.3 FM

Night owls, beware: the rec folk are contemplating putting the lights on a timer. The 'Til Dawn Lobby is getting geared up.

BLESSED EXCESS

In their name, Notre Dame students have taken jump shots in a blizzard, caused a roof to cave in, and called themselves unspeakable things like Roman Polanski's Babysitting Service, Bernhard Goetz and Four Guys Who Can't Shoot Either, and Indira Gandhi and the Sikhs Feet Underground. In short, they haven't exactly behaved in accordance with the ideals for which the Golden Dome has stood over the years. Then again, the Bookstore Basketball Tournament wasn't the work of Knute Rockne. It was birthed by a couple of fun-loving undergrads, Vince Meconi and Fritz Hoefer, who in 1972 risked their academic lives to start the five-on-five, all-weather, lose-and-you're-out bacchanal that has since become the centerpiece of Notre Dame's spring An Tostal festival. Bookstore, which is named for the campus concern next to the courts on which all the madness originally unfolded, has grown from a thin volume of 53 teams to an almost unmanageable 560-team tome.

Of course, as all veteran Bookstore Bennies know, sheer quantity pales before quality. People still talk about how John Shumate and Dwight Clay played on the first tourney titlists; how Tom Clements, the fabled Irish quarterback, once tossed in eight Js during a monsoon to cop the title for his team; how the snows (this is springtime in northern Indiana, after all) once brought all dribbling to a stop; how a throng of onlookers perched atop the Bookstore once collapsed its roof; and how Digger made sure the poles got padded after a varsity player busted his collarbone one year. (People *don't* talk about some of the team names that demented collegiate minds have come up with.)

Somehow, year after year, each successive tourney commissioner manages to dogleg a few more teams into the bracket, so there's no reason to doubt the participation of the entire student body one of these springs. That would result in roughly 9,000 maniacs, making up some 1,800 teams, playing hundreds and hundreds and hundreds of games. . . . But, as we said, the quality's the thing, not the quantity.

BOOKSTORE COURTS
NOTRE DAME UNIVERSITY
SOUTH BEND, INDIANA

 4/2      92.9 FM

The most storied, but certainly no longer the only, place to hoop it up in the shadow of the Dome. Other spots include Lyons Courts (two slabs) and Stepan Center, where a lot of Bookstore tournament games get played (eight slabs, plus lights). Sundays at ''The Rock''—Rockne Memorial

65

The Bookstore title game now gets run at Notre Dame's Stepan Center. (Can you find the University of Akron's football coach? Then again, do you want to find the University of Akron's football coach?) (Vincent Wehby, Jr.)

Gym—you'll find a lively oriental game. "No accident," confirms a regular. "That's when the computer center's closed." All campus pick-up is played according to Bookstore rules: games to twenty-one, win by two.

MARTIN LUTHER KING REC CENTER
1522 WEST LINDEN
SOUTH BEND, INDIANA

2/1
92.9 FM

"The Pride of the West Side" in South Bend. Even a few of Digger's charges make the trek over from time to time. A one-time habitué: Hill Street Bluesman and ex-UCLAn Mike Warren.

KIMBALL PARK
ROUTE 56
SPRINGS VALLEY, INDIANA

 2/1    104.7 FM

The quaintest little sign—HE PLAYED HERE AND HAD HIS FUN; THAT'S WHY STATE IS NUMBER ONE—*appeared here while homeboy Larry Bird made his mark at Indiana State. Since then, this spot has become positively shrinelike. Those who feel unworthy of J-ing on such hallowed ground may take themselves crosstown to West Baden Community Park.*

HYTE CENTER
13TH AND COLLEGE
TERRE HAUTE, INDIANA

4/2      107.5 FM

"The comp's pretty tight," says one of the many vets, who include lots *of farm kids in from the outskirts. Carl Nicks is a frequent visitor.*

TAPAWINGO PARK
LOWER SEARS PARKING LOT
WEST LAFAYETTE, INDIANA

 4/2      96.5 FM

Don your official Cheryl Tiegs hooping togs before hooking up in this run, back of the department store. Best runs summer evenings. Be sure you've been extended credit before calling any charges.

IOWA

BEYER HALL
IOWA STATE UNIVERSITY
AMES, IOWA

10/5

91.5 FM

The pick-up scene here can sparkle, especially when it's graced by the presence of the occasional slumming Cyclone. Like summer stock, an excellent mix of university students and community players.

KENWOOD SCHOOLYARD
3700 E, N.E.
CEDAR RAPIDS, IOWA

 4/2

103 FM

Summer evenings, beginning around 5:30, is when the shooting and scooting begins. Basketball bears hibernate over at Coe College during the winter.

PLAYLAND
NORTH 41ST AND B
COUNCIL BLUFFS, IOWA

 8/4

98 FM

Not a toy store, or an amusement park, or an adult social club—just an enormous rec complex, across the river from Omaha. All runs go to twenty-one.

GOOD PARK
17TH AND UNIVERSITY
DES MOINES, IOWA

 4/2   89.9 FM

The name does not stem from the quality of the neighborhood in which this place finds itself. Nor does the name do justice to the game, which is strictly B-A-D.

YMCA
101 LOCUST
DES MOINES, IOWA

10/5   89.9 FM

A mildly nerdy, non-rural type prevails here, where the only corn you'll find is on active feet. Was that "in your face" you heard? Nah . . . "interface."

DODGER COURTS
10TH AND 19TH
FORT DODGE, IOWA

 4/2   92 FM

You'll find a frequent smattering of women here, confirming the state's rep for distaff distinction.

FIELDHOUSE
UNIVERSITY OF IOWA
IOWA CITY, IOWA

26/11   100.7 FM

Few campus facilities can match the hospitality of this spot, where a strict open-gym policy prevails. (The feeling is—and we like the logic here—that the university is funded by the state, which is supported by the taxpayers, ergo. . . .) Gals don't just play often, but often play with the guys.

Iowa City *A Hawk's-Eye view of the action at the University of Iowa Fieldhouse, where even non-Hawks are free to fly in. (Byron Hetzler)*

IOWA CITY REC CENTER
BURLINGTON AND GILBERT
IOWA CITY, IOWA

4/2   93.9 FM

These courts are segregated—one's for chumps, the other for those with reps, including any Hawkeyes who can be wooed from campus.

MONROE MIDDLE SCHOOLYARD
12TH AND MONROE
MASON CITY, IOWA

 2/1    1490 AM

Ballplayers on the other side of town are loyal to another patriot's— John Adams's—middle school. The serious patch themselves into the summer league at North Iowa Community College.

KANSAS

BELL REC CENTER
3600 RAINBOW
KANSAS CITY, KANSAS

2/1 103.3 FM

Trini Lopez should have added a few bars about Bell when he crooned about K.C. women and K.C. wine. This is the main run in town, and home to the Metro Summer League.

MAHURON PARK
EAST 8TH AND CALVERT
LIBERAL, KANSAS

 2/1 108 FM

Always has had, and always will have, the best pick-up game in town. Check out the Sunday afternoon cricket game on the nearby field. Then again, don't *check out the Sunday afternoon cricket game on the nearby field.*

THE COP SHOP
ANTIOCH AND 87TH
OVERLAND PARK, KANSAS

 2/1 103.3 FM

The talent ranges widely at this spot, which attracts many blacks from the city and gets its name from the nearby police station. Check out the main homeboy, Harry the Helicopter, who always plays in painter's pants.

71

CITY HALL
805 MAIN
SABETHA, KANSAS

2/1    102 FM

The court is short and narrow; worse, the ceiling is low. But at least that low bridge is "live" (in play). Open from 8 A.M. to 10 P.M. every day.

MAIN GYM
KANSAS WESLEYAN UNIVERSITY
SALINA, KANSAS

6/3    99.9 FM

The noontime and evening games continue through the summer. The comp's good enough to induce the local small-college and juco coaches to stop by for occasional peeks.

HILLCREST COMMUNITY CENTER
21ST AND CALIFORNIA
TOPEKA, KANSAS

6/3    103.3 FM

This gem of a gym takes after the surname of director Jim Gorgeous, who swears he has never hosted a game show. Eastlawn and Central Park community centers are a little untidier, but definitely worth a look.

EMPORIA STREET PARK
EMPORIA AND 11TH
WICHITA, KANSAS

 2/1    103.7 FM

Not a whole lot has changed over the years, other than Darnell Valentine leaving for greener pastures. But this spot in an aircraft-industry town is still filled with frequent flyers.

72

LYNETTE WOODARD REC CENTER
18TH AND VOLUSTIA
WICHITA, KANSAS

2/1   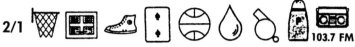 103.7 FM

In keeping with the spirit of the Center's Globetrotting namesake, gals don't play unless they can run with the guys.

KENTUCKY

BLUEGRASS BALL

From Pikeville to Paducah, this is basketball at its naturalistic finest, the way Dr. James envisioned it. It's the game out of doors, with Dirt Bowls and Dust Bowls and sundry other earthen receptacles, splendid and sociable. Check out the variety of hoops, and where they show up. There's a tire rim riveted to a tree. A mangled coat hanger over a carport. A Nerf hoop standing watch over the portal of a *dog* house, for goodness sake. No Old Kentucky Home *is* a home without one. They play half-court ball "straight up" all over this state, but it's the stretched-out summer stuff—at Shawnee, Douglass, and Kendall-Perkins parks—that glows.

CENTRAL PARK
CENTRAL AND 17TH
ASHLAND, KENTUCKY

 2/1   93 FM

Late afternoons draw good crowds. The ladies suit up for summer-league games, but rarely play pick-up.

PIERCE-FORD TOWER COURTS
WESTERN KENTUCKY UNIVERSITY
BOWLING GREEN, KENTUCKY

 16/8   1340 AM

Rare is the time at least one of the "Candy Stripe Goals" isn't in use. A nice town-gown mix, inasmuch as IDs aren't required.

LATONIA ELEMENTARY SCHOOLYARD
40TH AND HUNTINGTON
COVINGTON, KENTUCKY

 4/2    102 FM

A good sign: the nets here get replaced often. Gobel Park, across town on 3rd, services other Covingtonians with two slabs of its own.

EAST FRANKFORT PARK
MYRTLE AND VERSAILLES
FRANKFORT, KENTUCKY

 4/2    89.9 FM

If you don't want to make the twenty-mile trek to Lexington and Douglass Park's Herb Washington Arena—but believe us, you do want to make that journey sometime—a few Kentucky State football players may rope you into a game here.

WELDON PARK
CLEVELAND AND LESLIE
GLASGOW, KENTUCKY

 2/0    105.5 FM

More shooters than players here, though rec-league games bump the comp up a notch. School gyms (when they're open) attract Glasgow's best, so inquire where they be runnin' at.

Hopkinsville The bricks have long since been laid to rest at West Side Park, where Sunshine Lynch stages his Dirt Bowl. (Kentucky New Era)

WEST SIDE PARK
WEST 9TH AND SEVENTH
HOPKINSVILLE, KENTUCKY

 2/1
1370 AM

Known colloquially as Sunshine Arena, after Darryl (Sunshine) Lynch, founder and director of the Sunshine Dirt Bowl. The league not only has a Super Sunday of its own (the third in June; save the date), but has the gumption to invite other Dirt Bowls to J on the big day.

INEZ SCHOOLYARD
ROUTE 40
INEZ, KENTUCKY

 2/1
93.7 FM

The folks in Inez (pop. 450) are very serious about their ball, as the quality of this facility and the play attests. Postgame, tool up the street to Crum Motors for a pop from the machine and hoop talk with Frank.

Lexington *At Blazer Hall on campus, University of Kentucky undergrads are a quick study in the game of H-O-R-S-E.*

BLAZER HALL COURTS
UNIVERSITY OF KENTUCKY
LEXINGTON, KENTUCKY

 4/2   94.5 FM

Just a jump shot away from the Joe B. Hall Wildcat Lodge, and not much farther from a few of the less opulent outbuildings on campus. This being Kentucky, a lot of H-O-R-S-E gets played. In Memorial Coliseum across the way, join the noontime run with Cliff Hagan. He's still a happy hooker, and does a great Adolph Rupp imitation, mock–chewing out anyone missing a lay-up.

DOUGLASS PARK
GEORGETOWN AND HOWARD
LEXINGTON, KENTUCKY

 4/2   94.5 FM

Plan a visit to the Skydome ("The only roof is the sky") for that special day in July known as Dirt Bowl Super Sunday, when the legendary Pretty Pie, wearing his one-of-a-kind specs, steps out, and little Toot-Toot wails out the Anthem "in twelve different languages at the same time."

STELLA MOORE ATHLETIC FIELD
HIGHWAY 23
LOUISA, KENTUCKY

 2/1   105 FM

The Baron would love the game here: nothing but white boys playing run 'n' gun. Weekly three-on-three tournaments take place throughout the summer.

CRAWFORD GYM
UNIVERSITY OF LOUISVILLE
LOUISVILLE, KENTUCKY

 6/3   95.7 FM

There are so many places, and so many players, in the 'Ville, that the action is a movable feast. It whistle-stops here on Monday and Thursday nights.

MELVIN & MELVIN

Melvin Boyd Cunningham vividly remembers the moment he first saw Melvin (The Dipper) Turpin. It was in a Lexington, Kentucky, park, and Turpin was a 6′10″, 201-pound teenage thyroid case who begged the question, "Do you play basketball?" Cunningham *asked* the question, and thus began a most remarkable relationship.

"I don't like the game," Turpin replied. Turned out that he didn't *know* the game. So Cunningham set about teaching it, from the three-second rule on up. Turpin went on to pick up a few more pointers, many more pounds, and All-America honors at Kentucky; Cunningham, with sidekick Herb Washington, continued to reach out to Lexington youngsters, showcasing them for college coaches through the storied Dirt Bowl league.

Beginning in 1967 the Dirt Bowl was run outdoors on the clay tennis courts of Douglass Park, from which it derives its name. Ten years later two sealed slabs went in, adorned at each end with concrete dinosaur-necked supports. Melvin Boyd bowed out soon thereafter, but he still keeps tabs on his 265-pound charge—and pulls tabs off of pop-top cans. If the shot on the previous page is any indication, the Dipper has taught his tutor a thing or two, too.

As Melvin Turpin can attest, things go better with Douglass Park denizen Melvin Boyd Cunningham. (Bill Luster)

SHAWNEE PARK
WESTERN AND MARKET
LOUISVILLE, KENTUCKY

 8/4      1350 AM

The granddaddy of Dirt Bowls, sho'nuff major league. Pick-up play goes on year-round; league play—with junior, senior, and open divisions—is a June-to-August ritual in the 'Ville.

CITY PARK
168 EAST MAIN
MOREHEAD, KENTUCKY

 4/2      1330 AM

Mostly half court; the better players make the trip to Lexington—the drive is forty minutes—for a chance to stretch it out.

NORTH GYM
MURRAY STATE UNIVERSITY
MURRAY, KENTUCKY

8/4      100.3 FM

Be on the lookout for Mike Ridley and his Gorillas, an informal not-so-pick-up pick-up team led by a dentist who played for Western Kentucky in the early '60s. You'll open wide and say "aaaah."

KENDALL-PERKINS PARK
WEST 5TH AND ORCHARD
OWENSBORO, KENTUCKY

 4/2   96 FM

They call their eight-day tourney here the Dust Bowl, because Louisville and Lexington call theirs Dirt Bowls, and Owensboro wants to be different. Regulars may play pick-up on Tuesdays and Thursdays, but, as league director Jerry says, "like in the pros, Wednesday's your 'travel' day." Come winter, check out the indoor Chatauqua Center crosstown.

BOB AMOS PARK
CEDAR GAP
PIKEVILLE, KENTUCKY

 2/1

1240 AM

If you feel like taking a few laps to loosen up, no problem—there's a full track adjacent to the court. Games start picking up around 6 on summer evenings.

CLEAR CREEK PARK
SEVENTH
SHELBYVILLE, KENTUCKY

 4/2

940 AM

With only one court lit, there's occasionally a wait when rockfish like Charles Hurt and Mike Casey happen by and the runs get serious. The water fountain is over by the tennis court; more potent libations can be had from the friendly folks at Clear Creek Liquors.

LOUISIANA

CHEATHAM PARK
JONES AND BROADWAY
ALEXANDRIA, LOUISIANA

 4/2   92 FM

Summertime action begins at 10 A.M., every day of the week, and runs 'til sundown. Not uncommon to find the occasional Southwest Conference ex playing here.

ANNA JORDAN REC CENTER
STILT
BATON ROUGE, LOUISIANA

2/1   101.5 FM

Near the Southern U. campus, this spot attracts a lot of current and former Jaguars, along with the best noirs of Baton Rouge. If your nickname is Gravity or Glue, geaux (that's how they spell go down here) elsewhere. The leagues run out of City Park Rec Center, the ladies out of Antioch and Sharon Hills.

THE SLAB
1811 JOHNSON
LAFAYETTE, LOUISIANA

 4/2   1330 AM

One court has rims at regulation; the other has 8' fantasy goals. Games start at noon, and the play heats up as the sun goes down.

81

Lafayette *Like Andrew Toney, you can cut your teeth on the best ball in southwest Louisiana at The Slab. (Brad Kemp)*

MEMORIAL GYM
MCNEESE STATE UNIVERSITY
LAKE CHARLES, LOUISIANA

8/4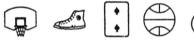
1300 AM

One-on-one and three-on-three are played Chicago—five buckets win and losers sit. With all the throwing down going down, the authorities have wisely installed collapsible rims.

SAUL ADLER REC CENTER
WESTMINSTER AND LUKE
MONROE, LOUISIANA

6/3
98.3 FM

Just execute a pull? (That's preferable, you'll recall, to merely "getting a rebound.") Give a look downcourt; you may see NFL speedman Sammy White breaking long.

ROSENWALD CENTER
EARHART AND BROAD
NEW ORLEANS, LOUISIANA

6/3
98.5 FM

A remodeled gym in a housing project, with good comp that's less glitzy than what you'll find at Shakespeare. Three-day-long open tournaments are held throughout the year; free-play is from 6 to 9 in the evenings.

SHAKESPEARE PARK
WASHINGTON AND LASALLE
NEW ORLEANS, LOUISIANA

 4/2   98.5 FM

To be or not to be? This spot most definitely be. All of the city's best pass through. The courts feature a roof, so runs run through driving rain and brutal sun.

LAMBRIGHT CENTER
LOUISIANA TECH UNIVERSITY
RUSTON, LOUISIANA

16/8   98 FM

There are two gyms here, ''red'' and ''blue,'' each with eight racks. Games go to fifteen by ones. As you play, pay tribute to local product Karl (Mailman) Malone, and let nothing stay you in the swift execution of your appointed bounds.

AIRPORT PARK
KENNEDY
SHREVEPORT, LOUISIANA

6/3   92 FM

Please get clearance from the tower before dunking. Also, check out the three full courts outdoors, and the downtown court at Hearn, across from the hospital. Hackers and businessmen would do best to try the Y.

STOTHER COURT
NICHOLLS STATE UNIVERSITY
THIBODAUX, LOUISIANA

 2/1      98.5 FM

Handmade backboards and a dirt floor give this spot a down-home charm. Boxes abound, and prospective players perch like crows on the sidelines.

MAINE

HASTY COMMUNITY CENTER
GAMAGE
AUBURN, MAINE

6/3

This is the don't-call-us, we'll-call-you school of pick-up: you register your name and phone number, and they give you a ring and an assignment in their 11:30-to-1:30 lunch slot.

WILLIAMS PLAYGROUND
BANGOR AND QUIMBY
AUGUSTA, MAINE

 2/1

While the women air it out over on Gage Street, Augusta's men's league has taken care of business for twenty-two years here, at one of the state's first lighted outdoor courts. Hit the Y for indoor play.

DAKIN PARK
BROADWAY AND STILLWATER
BANGOR, MAINE

 2/1

Lights blaze 'til 10 and bubblers gurgle 'til 6. The nets? "They come and go," says a Parks and Rec type. Another run worth checking out is at Fairmount Terrace Park, over on 13th and Union.

*What's in a name?
R-E-S-P-E-C-T. (Project
Respect)*

BOOTH BAY REGION YMCA
TOWNSEND
BOOTH BAY HARBOR, MAINE

6/3  **91.9 FM**

*The comp gets cranked up come summer, when vacationing collegians
happen by. Monday and Wednesday nights are set aside for ball.*

REC CENTER
BENNETT AND NORTH
CARIBOU, MAINE

2/1  **600 AM**

*The bros come in from nearby Loring AFB. Hoops is so big in the
northernmost reaches of this state that the many leagues here—and across
the street at Teague Park in the summer—fill up quickly.*

MEMORIAL ARMORY
65 CENTRAL
LEWISTON, MAINE

10/5  **1470 AM**

*A core group of regulars runs Saturday afternoons, and weekday eve-
nings 6 to 9.*

85

THE NAME GAME

We know it's tough, what with NBA already taken. But couldn't more leagues get hip to the fact that there are many ways to name a hoop loop, other than after a town, facility, or corporate sponsor?

Consider the more inspired examples. Folks in Indiana and Kentucky call their leagues *bowls*. Dirt Bowls and Dust Bowls aren't football games played on snowless New Year's Days, but hoary institutions, named for the earthen ancestors of latter-day, blacktop-covered slabs.

Other leagues take the name of a special, celebrated someone, like Connie Hawkins in Pittsburgh and Randy Smith in Buffalo. Sometimes these individuals are chosen for having provided the spirit (Holcombe Rucker in Harlem and Charles Baker in Philadelphia), and sometimes for having provided the financial wherewithal (James Bailey in Boston). But occasionally they're cited for hardly any reason at all. A few basketball Bennies in Queens began the Ray Felix League in the '50s simply in honor of Felix, then a Knicks rookie, moving into their neighborhood. Teddy Lilakos (Portsmouth, New Hampshire), Priscilla Abruzza (Philly), Wayne Robinson (Greensboro, North Carolina), Nathan Bill (Springfield, Massachusetts), Freddie Summer (Gambier, Ohio), and Floyd Theard (Denver, Colorado) all have leagues named in their honor—but they are very local heroes, utterly obscure to everyone but their homeboys.

The most savory league names, however, are the ones that resonate with urban self-help and civic utopianism. They can make the pronouncements of Jesse Jackson seem clichéd by comparison, and are well represented on the following In-Your-Face hit parade of summer-league titles:

Warning: We Must Respect Each Other League *(Milwaukee)*

Soul in the Hole Tournament *(Brooklyn)*

I.M.A.G.E. Future Stars League *(Louisville)*

Netpoppers Inner-City League *(Tulsa)*

Hot Nets League *(Atlanta)*

Ebony and Ivory League *(Boston)*

Sunshine Dirt Bowl League *(Hopkinsville, Ky.)*

Project Survival League *(Baltimore)*

Operation Positive League *(Canton, Ohio)*

Joint Effort League *(Denver)*

Rabbit League *(Freehold, New Jersey)*

Shoot Straight Park League *(Uncasville, Connecticut)*

Uptown League *(Atlantic City)*

League of Champions *(Wichita)*

DEERING OAKS PARK
DEERING AND PARK
PORTLAND, MAINE

 2/1

As a result of the increased use this facility has gotten (from sailors at the nearby Navy base, plus Vietnamese and Cambodian refugees), a resurfacing job is in the offing. So are an additional court and new lights.

MILTON GRANT OUTDOOR POOL AREA COURT
MAIN
PRESQUE ISLE, MAINE

 2/1

Mid-May 'til Labor Day the hanging out is serious here. Off-season weekends, check out the P.I. Rec Center.

MEMORIAL GYM
UNIVERSITY OF MAINE
ORONO, MAINE

6/3

Called ''The Pit''—and boy, is it. The place reeks of sweat socks and history.

ELLIS PARK
OCEAN
YORK BEACH, MAINE

 2/1

The fee you pay to park in the adjacent lot goes toward court upkeep. A worthy cause, inasmuch as the nets have to be replaced every three weeks during the summer.

MARYLAND

HILLSDALE ELEMENTARY SCHOOLYARD
ROUTE 40 AND EDMUND
ABERDEEN, MARYLAND

 4/2    **1190 AM**

About the only place in town where the backboards are still up. Father Time does as much damage as the slam-jammers.

MADISON SQUARE REC CENTER
BIDDLE AND EDEN
BALTIMORE, MARYLAND

8/4      **102.7 FM**

What Madison Square was to college hoops in the Apple, Madison Square is to pick-up in Crabtown: an obligatory stop. Ask anyone at any corner in town for directions to The Dome, and don't let the decaying neighborhood put you off. Fashion tip: wear coaching shorts with those deep pockets. They're popular in these parts.

MAPLEWOOD–ALTA VISTA REC CENTER
ALTA VISTA AND BALFOUR
BETHESDA, MARYLAND

 4/2      **107.3 FM**

Yup, the crowd that shows for the pick-up is affluent. But the summer league still attracts a very respectable sort of player.

NORTH GYM
UNIVERSITY OF MARYLAND
COLLEGE PARK, MARYLAND

6/3   88.1 FM

It's said that five alums, aged forty to fifty-five, never lose. Undergrads hoping to run may have to wait 'til mandatory retirement forces these winners out.

CENTRAL YMCA
QUEEN CITY AND BALTIMORE
CUMBERLAND, MARYLAND

6/3   106.1 FM

Kids here grow up wanting to run for local power Allegheny Community College; then they return to the Y to remember their roots.

Bethesda *The wood at Maplewood–Alta Vista catches a rare summer breather. (Mitchell Layton)*

89

41ST STREET COURTS
41ST AND COASTAL
OCEAN CITY, MARYLAND

8/4   104 FM

The games here (to sixteen) are played at rims with uneven heights, so sides swap hoops when one team reaches eight.

DOVERDALE PARK
BROWN
SALISBURY, MARYLAND

 2/1      1470 AM

The Maggs Center at Salisbury State is the indoor alternative to this spot, which is pretty spartan: no leagues, no lights, no libations, no ladies.

ROCK CREEK REC CENTER
MEADOWBROOK
SILVER SPRING, MARYLAND

 6/3   107.3 FM

Known to the locals as Candy Cane City because of the barber-pole stripes on the rack sticks. Be sure to bring quarters for the lights if you plan on playing at night.

SILGO CREEK PARK
SILGO CREEK
WHEATON, MARYLAND

 6/3   100.1 FM

The setting may be pastoral, but the high profanity level tells a truer story. Earmuffs suggested for the faint of heart.

MASSACHUSETTS

THE HORSESHOE
UNIVERSITY OF MASSACHUSETTS
AMHERST, MASSACHUSETTS

 4/2      91.1 FM

Check out Funkathon Weekend every April, when pick-up teams play a tournament under the sun, then groove on concert jams under the stars.

PERRY COURT
81 DASCOMB
ANDOVER, MASSACHUSETTS

 2/1      103 FM

There are only nine ready players in the Perry family, so someone will always be looking for a fifth. The Rose Glen Ice Cream Shop is just down the street; tradition holds that losers spring for the frappes.

THE HUB

Hoops has been a major source of progress in one of the country's most troubled cities. The Boston Neighborhood Basketball League acknowledges the city's polarities by giving each Beantown bailiwick its own division; then it throws the best from each into the cauldron of the play-offs, where there hasn't been an incident to speak of in almost two decades. A younger loop, the Ebony-Ivory League on the Fenway, has been just as progressive, helping to clean up a stately and historical but untidy part of town. Both leagues are first rate, but ever since the advent of Patrick Ewing—and an ambitious court-building program undertaken by the Cambridge city fathers—the pick-up power has shifted perceptibly across the river.

CITY HOSPITAL GYM
55 NORTHAMPTON
BOSTON, MASSACHUSETTS

2/1.
88.9 FM

Most of the players are hospital employees, but for three bucks anybody can intern.

DERBY PARK
WASHINGTON AND NORTHAMPTON
BOSTON, MASSACHUSETTS

 8/4
1090 AM

No place for strangers. Reefer is practically legal here. Beantown's finest have been known to interrupt games to search players for contraband.

ROBERTO CLEMENTE PARK
PARK AND JERSEY ON THE FENS
BOSTON, MASSACHUSETTS

 4/2
108 FM

A game here is serious stuff. Consider: (1) the halfway house across the street contributes players and spectators alike; (2) the Ebony-Ivory League, whose games are played here, has a T-shirt that boasts, without hyperbole, OUR RUN IS NO. 1; *and (3) the most expensive hot-dog vendor in the city works here.*

WASHINGTON PARK
WASHINGTON AND MARTIN LUTHER KING
BOSTON, MASSACHUSETTS

 6/3
1090 AM

Wash Park has had a mystique ever since the early '70s, when several Celtics used to come around. Now the runs on the boulevard include indoor action at the adjacent Shelburne Rec Center. Says a Cantabridgian from across the river, charitably, "They argue too much, but it's definitely good ball."

THE BEAN

"I'm ready to slow down a little bit," says Al Brodsky, who's still known to ferry Boston ballplayers from run to run in his '62 Cadillac Fleetwood limousine. It all began when the Roxbury drugstore where he worked as a soda jerk was torn down and replaced by a spanking new Y. So Brodsky began whipping up frappes of power forwards and lead guards, venturing into the most forbidding housing projects to recruit his players. "The hardcore kids"—he shrugs—"seemed to be my better ballplayers."

Though an accountant by trade, Brodsky will struggle when asked to total up all the Boston Neighborhood Basketball League titles he and his Titans have won since the BNBL began more than fifteen years ago. "It's five nineteen-and-under championships," he says with certainty. "And seven or eight fifteen-and-unders," he adds, more hesitantly. Whatever the exact figures, Brodsky is far and away the winningest coach in that illustrious league's history of promoting Hub hoops and defusing racial tensions. "Bean *is* Boston," says one Roxburyan. "I mean, he's kin to the Kennedys."

The Bean (he's the guy with the clean bean) and his classic have ride chauffered more Cadillac ballplayers from run to run than the odometer can remember. (Stephanie Wolff)

Boston *At Wash Park you don't stop and pop, but take your man to the cleaners.* (Stephanie Wolff)

CRESCENT COURT
CRESCENT
BROCKTON, MASSACHUSETTS

 4/2
1090 AM

Smack-dab in the projects, with a rigid house rule regarding what constitutes a foul: absolutely, as Edwin Starr would say, nuthin'.

RIVERSIDE PRESS PARK
MEMORIAL AND RIVER
CAMBRIDGE, MASSACHUSETTS

 4/2
108 FM

Built in '81, this spot isn't exactly where Patrick Ewing grew up, but it's where he chooses to hang when he comes home. Press Park is note-worthy for Better Homes & Gardens *landscaping, ''straight-up'' on all half-court games, and the firm distinction between the run on the main court (a.k.a. The Parquet) and the B-level run next to it. Some players will sit through three or four games for a run on the main drag, rather than take an immediate spot in the B game.*

ROBERTS CENTER
BOSTON COLLEGE
CHESTNUT HILL, MASSACHUSETTS

6/3      **108 FM**

Best runs Tuesday and Thursday nights—except for three rarefied weeks in the early fall before NBA camps open, when many Celtics go informally during the afternoons. Look for Doug (Magic) Flutie playing his favorite sport.

SZOT PARK
FRONT
CHICOPEE, MASSACHUSETTS

 4/2      **107 FM**

This is an early-season spot, with highlights in the late spring and early summer. Those who come by later won't find as much jump-szooting going on.

FALMOUTH HEIGHTS COURT
ON-THE-BEACH
FALMOUTH HEIGHTS, MASSACHUSETTS

 2/1      **101.9 FM**

Though many locals rock at one of the schoolyards, the prime sunshine run is found here. Girls go in the mornings, guys after midday. There's a strip of ice-cream and grinder (that's New England for submarine) shops nearby.

Cambridge *These stragglers wouldn't be dogging it if they were running one court over, on Riverside Press Park's parquet.*

KENNEDY MEMORIAL RINK
BEARSES
HYANNIS, MASSACHUSETTS

6/3

A portable wood floor converts this spot from an ice rink to a hoop haven each summer. Most of the players were born before JFK took office.

SOUTH COMMON
BISHOP MARKHAM HOUSING PROJECT
LOWELL, MASSACHUSETTS

 4/2

980 AM

Ask about the popular indigenous game, a derivative of 21, called "Free." A terrific local high-school program ushers kids from here through the ranks to big-time ball.

NANTUCKET HIGH SCHOOLYARD
ATLANTIC AND SPARKS
NANTUCKET, MASSACHUSETTS

 2/1

106.1 FM

Mike Dunleavy no longer shows, but you can still find a whale of a run here, especially at the height of the tourist season. The core of the clientele: college kids with jobs on the island.

BUTLER PARK
ROCKDALE AND HAWTHORNE
NEW BEDFORD, MASSACHUSETTS

 6/3

1340 AM

You can see the steam rising from this spot between April and October. You'll find the best comp on the court closest to the zoo. (Please don't feed the animals.) The bros run at Monte Playground, at Acushnet and Purchase; the casual types at Hazlewood, near the shore.

FALLON FIELD
WALWORTH AND WALTER
ROSLINDALE, MASSACHUSETTS

 4/2   **108 FM**

The Home Market, fifty yards away on Roslindale, provides refreshments. Beware the German shepherd that pops balls with his teeth.

SACRED HEART SCHOOLYARD
SOUTH MAIN AND BEACH
SHARON, MASSACHUSETTS

  2/1   **108 FM**

Lights burn 'til about 10:30 P.M. in the summer. Cool off with the hoses by the Public Garden.

ACCESS ROAD COURTS
ACCESS
SOUTH DENNIS, MASSACHUSETTS

 6/3   **104 FM**

Home port for the All-Cape League, Cape Cod's kingfish summer loop. A local cable outlet picks up some of the action.

DR. JAS., DR. J, AND MR. J

The site of the first pick-up game could use a little picking-up. It's now a glass-strewn parking lot in the blighted Winchester Square section of Springfield. But just a few steps away, right around the corner from where that seminal YMCA gym once stood, you'll find the Dunbar Community Center, a hoary edifice that does justice to Dr. James Naismith's peach baskets and the bushels of madness they gave life to.

Dunbar was once the First South Church of Christ. Now a gym floor lies where the nave once did. Murals painted in bright pastels make do for the long-gone stained glass. And executive director Bob Jennings ministers to one of the community's most fundamental spiritual needs. Years ago, Jennings took on a young University of Massachusetts work-study intern named Julius Erving to help him run the gym. Today, when he isn't out begging funds and equipment to keep Dunbar open, Jennings, who's in his sixties, goes full court with the kids. "They'll say, 'Run with us, Mr. J.' I'll wake up the next morning a little stiffer. But I won't play half court. You stand around too much."

The holiest court in America sits just steps away from the game's birthplace in Springfield. Dunbar director Mr. J once had a Doctor for an intern. (Manny Millan)

DUNBAR COMMUNITY CENTER
OAK AND UNION
SPRINGFIELD, MASSACHUSETTS

4/1 91.9 FM

Mr. J, with aide de camp *Big Will, sets aside the 3-to-5 after-school hours for teens. The court is called Death Valley, for reasons you may not live to tell.*

COUSY COURT
HARDING
WORCESTER, MASSACHUSETTS

 2/1  107.3 FM

Located in Crompton Park, the court has undergone a major overhaul. But the better players are still white, and behind-the-back passes are still in vogue. There's also, as the Cooz would say in his inimitable way, a vewy good weague.

MICHIGAN

INTRAMURAL BUILDING
UNIVERSITY OF MICHIGAN
ANN ARBOR, MICHIGAN

10/5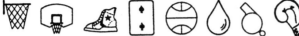
103 FM

This isn't just a no-autopsy, no-foul facility; it's a B.Y.O.F.—Bring Your Own Formaldehyde—kind of place. When guys from Detroit and Chicago are up, and some of the locals turn out, and the finest from campus show, the I.M. sparkles.

CIVIC CENTER
MICHIGAN AND GREENFIELD
DEARBORN, MICHIGAN

4/2
101.1 FM

The playroom for this Motown bedroom community, where there always seems to be some sort of run in progress. Drop by any weekday, 12 to 5, for the best.

FRANKLIN WRIGHT SETTLEMENT
ELMWOOD AND CHARLEVOIX
DETROIT, MICHIGAN

6/3
107.5 FM

Things rarely settle down at this spot, which services one of the country's oldest settlement houses. The gym is occasionally blessed by Isiah Thomas. Five outdoor slabs await you at Belle Isle Park.

Detroit *Ceciliaville has seen its share of diamonds, but even the diamonds in the rough turn in a gem now and then. (Blake Discher)*

PALMER PARK
WOODWARD
DETROIT, MICHIGAN

 2/1   105.9 FM

May be the Motor City's best outdoor pick-up spot. Games are straight, which can't be said for many of the nonhooping males who populate the park and also find it a great pick-up spot.

ST. CECILIA REC CENTER
BURLINGAME AND GRAND RIVER
DETROIT, MICHIGAN

2/1

105.9 FM

Ceciliaville, as it's known, is a municipality with no limits to speak of, as occasional visits from Magic and Isiah have demonstrated. Sam Washington is the Godfather here, the man in charge. The other Motor City must-see: the Brewster Rec Center, which serves the projects on whose corners the Supremes and Four Tops came up.

VALLEY COURT PARK
GRAND RIVER AND MICHIGAN
EAST LANSING, MICHIGAN

 2/1

730 AM

This park, which enjoyed its heyday in the late '70s, could use some Earvin renewal, which it gets whenever the Magic Man comes home. Otherwise, the action is pretty Spartan.

BALLENGER PARK
GRAND TRAVERSE AND 5TH
FLINT, MICHIGAN

 4/2

92.7 FM

The runs get bumped up a notch on summer Sundays. Berston Field House provides more reliable quality control throughout the week, with all-name supe Justice Thigpen keeping order on the court.

MARTIN LUTHER KING PARK
FRANKLIN AND FULLER
GRAND RAPIDS, MICHIGAN

 10/5

1140 AM

Because Grand Rapids is on the fringe of the Eastern time zone, you can play here during the summer without lights 'til close to 10 P.M. Great sideshows, including L. E. Brisbin, pastor of the Apostolic Faith Church, who makes sideline imprecations to the hooping masses to watch his ''Message of Hope'' telecasts on Sunday mornings; and hip-hop honcho Robert S., who says, ''I put the rap in Grand Rapids.''

IN YOUR FACE, AT YOUR DOORSTEP

The numbers say it all: thousands of people playing hundreds of games of three-on-three over five blocks on three streets during three days in July in a sleepy west Michigan town. The town is Lowell, and the event is (we'll give you the AM-radio version) The Gus Macker All-World Invitational 3-on-3 Outdoor Backyard Basketball Tournament, the first and most fabulous of its kind. Male and female, old and young, black and white, good and lousy go at it in the spirit of the Macker motto: "Wear a Macker smile for all the world to see; Macker makes the world a better place to be." They listen to the tunes of Disko Bob. They peruse the Mackerville *Gusette.* They keep their eyes pealed for the leprechaun-like Scott McNeal, whom somebody gave the nickname "Gus Macker," for no apparent reason, in the seventh grade, and in whose driveway the entire insanity began in 1974.

"Everybody thinks Gus Macker is a 6'8" black guy," says Gus. "I'm 5'7", and that's stretching it." He's also a white guy, though his mom, noting his passion for ribs, sometimes wonders. "He's a Gemini, you know," Mama Macker says. "Split personality."

MACKER DRIVEWAY
521 ELIZABETH
LOWELL, MICHIGAN

 1/6

1140 AM

Where Macker Mania began over one memorable spring break long ago. Renee Macker, Mrs. Gus, is among the ladies who hoop it up. Deal some digits to neighbors Orloe and Mary Anne Gwatkin; they hip.

Lowell gussies up for the annual three-day hoopathon (facing page) spawned by the munchkinlike Macker Man (left). (Bill Eppridge)

WALLACE E. HOLLAND COMMUNITY CENTER
EAST AND SOUTH
PONTIAC, MICHIGAN

2/1

97.9 FM

We considered subbing a football helmet for the boxing glove symbol, because William Gay and sundry Detroit Lions work out here.

CIVITAN REC CENTER
3RD AND WADSWORTH
SAGINAW, MICHIGAN

4/2

107.1 FM

They've been packing the place for more than thirty years, and it's still the only spot in town with a hardwood floor. Worth the trip, even if you have to pull a Simon & Garfunkel and hitchhike four days. A newer gym, the First Ward Community Center on North 12th, gets plenty of use, too.

MINNESOTA

ST. STEPHEN HOME
84TH AND FRANCE
BLOOMINGTON, MINNESOTA

 2/1   89.9 FM

Interns working at this home for the mentally retarded have generated a serious rep for the court. Chumps who stumble by may find ''The Institute'' court a school for higher learning.

Bloomington *You'll end up paying if you don't pay the staff at St. Stephen Home any mind; most can hold their own on the court out back. (Mike McCollow)*

SAUNDERS GARDEN
1420 WEST 98½
BLOOMINGTON, MINNESOTA

 1/0
89.9 FM

Home to the Saunders Hoop Invitational Tournament, a.k.a. The S.H.I.T., each July. It's not obscene; just obsessive. Take S.H.I.T. fix-ture Ross Rislove, who spends the better part of June gearing up for the double-elimination, two-on-two event by—pardon our French—eating, drinking, and sleeping S.H.I.T. He even talks S.H.I.T. to anyone who'll listen (a dwindling number, to be sure, as tourney time draws near). Said Rislove, on hearing that Celtics star Kevin McHale might enter the S.H.I.T. after Boston had been bounced from the NBA playoffs: ''Don't want no runner-up on my team.''

JEWISH EDUCATIONAL CENTER
1602 EAST 2ND
DULUTH, MINNESOTA

 4/2
102 FM

The action here has been known to heat up—on those rare occasions when the temperature gets above freezing.

MARTIN LUTHER KING PARK
42ND AND NICOLLET
MINNEAPOLIS, MINNESOTA

 2/1
89.9 FM

Some of the biggest mosquitoes in the civilized world put on a full-court press at dusk, making strict adherence to the converse of Meminger's Law—if you don't hang out, you can't play ball—tough.

NORTH COMMONS COMMUNITY CENTER
16TH AND MORGAN
MINNEAPOLIS, MINNESOTA

 4/2
89.9 FM

For winter play there's a nearby full gym, which once accommodated not-so-gentle Ben Coleman, the former Goph and Maryland Terp.

POWDERHORN PARK
34TH AND FIFTEENTH
MINNEAPOLIS, MINNESOTA

 2/1   89.9 FM

Pop the Purple Rain *soundtrack into your box when you play here to let locals know you're hip to His Royal Badness. Prince played his ball at nearby Bryant Junior High.*

NEMZEK HALL
MOORHEAD STATE UNIVERSITY
MOORHEAD, MINNESOTA

16/8   1280 AM

There's no finer place to run hereabouts. Three gyms often attract comp that, in turn, attracts the gawkers.

SPORTS AND REC CENTER
BETHEL COLLEGE
ST. PAUL, MINNESOTA

10/5   95 FM

It's been argued that more Minnesotans do their dog days hooping here than anywhere else in the state. With more than 1,000 enrolled in the summer league, it's probably true.

MISSISSIPPI

JOHN HENRY BEEK PARK
NIXON
BILOXI, MISSISSIPPI

 2/1   1240 AM

Action at Beek peaked recently, when the roof got blown off Biloxi's most popular indoor spot, the Division Street Community Center. The roof's back in place there, but a respectable crowd still shows here.

GET RID OF YOUR LID

In our first go-round, we included a chapter entitled "When in Rome." It pointed out how codes of behavior vary from court to court, and that it behooves each of us to adjust accordingly. Most of our counsel was fairly obvious, Coppertone-shouldn't-advertise-in-*Ebony*-type stuff. But there was one peculiar regional custom we neglected to mention: the rule, pervasive in the South, that prohibits anything but a bare head from entering a gym.

NO HATS WORN INSIDE GYM admonishes a notice in Tompkins Rec Center in Savannah. NO HAIR PICKS is the message glowering from the wall at Montgomery's Bellingrath Community Center. NO HEADWEAR IN GYM warns another sign, this one in the gym at Douglass High in Atlanta. Whence came these peculiar ordinances? "It's just a rule, come down from the supervisor," says Tompkins's Mike Pringle. "Guess they're trying to make gentlemen out of everybody."

Then again, a check at the Maple Street Park Gym in Rome, Georgia, reveals no such legislation. As we were saying, when in Rome . . .

107

Southern manners hold that a gentleman tip his hat to more than just a lady. At Tompkins, director Mike Pringle makes sure of it. (Stephen T. Frazier)

WALTER SILLERS COLISEUM
DELTA STATE UNIVERSITY
CLEVELAND, MISSISSIPPI

6/3  **106 FM**

A lenient coaching staff lets the townies have carte blanche, perhaps in the hope that someone special will take a liking to the school. Considering Del State's history as a power during the salad days of women's hoops, more girls should be playing.

STRANGE PARK
EAST WALKER
GREENVILLE, MISSISSIPPI

 2/1  **100.7 FM**

Blacks play make it, take it; whites don't. For indoor action, tool your ride by Wards, Rounds, or Covington rec centers.

GASTON HEWES REC CENTER
2608 17TH
GULFPORT, MISSISSIPPI

2/1  **1240 AM**

Be sure to bring a ball; the center doesn't have one.

SPORTS ARENA
UNIVERSITY OF SOUTHERN MISSISSIPPI
HATTIESBURG, MISSISSIPPI

8/4 **1580 AM**

The talent ranges from hard-core hackers to legitimate schoolboy prospects.

WHITE ROCK GYM
COUNTRY CLUB AND CLINTON
JACKSON, MISSISSIPPI

6/3 **94 FM**

The rocking isn't so white at White Rock. In fact, this spot is curiously situated on Country Club. A more balanced racial mix will be found at Sykes Gym, while the runs at Jackson State's Williams Center can always be counted on.

MCCARTHY GYM
MISSISSIPPI STATE UNIVERSITY
STARKVILLE, MISSISSIPPI

4/2 **106 FM**

The roof leaks, so beware the incipient warped spots, especially around the line at the No. 3 goal. And if it's a Saturday, be prepared to run off the table tennis types.

JACKSON STREET YMCA
JACKSON AND WALNUT
VICKSBURG, MISSISSIPPI

2/1 **99 FM**

SuperSonic Michael Phelps, once a star at Alcorn State, put his game together here while coming up. He returns for tune-ups each off-season. Games run to twenty-four by twos.

MISSOURI

ARENA PARK
NORTH KINGS AND WEST CAPE ROCK
CAPE GIRARDEAU, MISSOURI

  2/1   100.7 FM

The ''arena'' in the name is wishful thinking, though the park gets plenty of use just the same. The real arena—at least for the Cape summer league—is the Bubble over at Southeast Missouri State.

CRYSTAL CITY PARK
15TH AND NORTH JEFFERSON
CRYSTAL CITY, MISSOURI

 4/2    107.7 FM

In the town where Bill Bradley grew up, dribbling around chairs, you can find animate opponents. Also check out Hickory White Park.

ADMIRAL COONTZ REC CENTER
BROADWAY AND 79TH
HANNIBAL, MISSOURI

 4/2      92.9 FM

This spot was once a camp for German P.O.W.s, so an eleven-foot-high fence surrounds the gym. The play is O.K., but don't hold your breath waiting for a leaper who can touch the top of the wall.

Cape Girardeau *Hats may be taboo in much of the indoor South, but guys are free to frame their faces in the wide-open spaces of the Midwest, like Arena Park. (Pat Patterson)*

SHAWNEE MISSION NORTH HIGH SCHOOLYARD
JOHNSON AND METCALF
KANSAS CITY, MISSOURI

 2/1    103.3 FM

Set in a glen of trees, this court offers plenty of shade and protection from the wind. Still, a surfeit of hackers keeps conditions less than ideal.

MINOR SMITH PARK
81ST AND ASH
RAYTOWN, MISSOURI

 1/0      101.5 FM

Half court only, with the most serious play taking place under the lights. An adjacent volleyball court serves those who must wait.

111

JOHN LUCAS SR. COMPLEX
18TH AND ANGELIC
ST. JOSEPH, MISSOURI

 8/4   1550 AM

The place to pop the pill in aspirin town. This is hoop central, just across the street from Eastside Rec Center, where all the winter running gets done.

WOHL COMMUNITY CENTER
NORTH KINGS
ST. LOUIS, MISSOURI

2/1   1600 AM

The summertime play here is first-rate, though more gutbucket than the runs over at St. Louis U.—and more likely to feature a pro cameo.

O'REILLY GYM
GLENSTONE AND DIVISION
SPRINGFIELD, MISSOURI

6/3   98.7 FM

You ease yourself into a run here. First, you amble by the so-called "challenge" court and get yourself signed up. Then you get the blood flowing with a game of handball next door. Summers, the gym closes down, this being a softball town.

"Ever play this game, Chief? C'mon, I'll show ya. Old Indian game. It's called, uh, put the ball in the hole." —*Jack Nicholson to Will Sampson in* One Flew Over the Cuckoo's Nest. *(Copyright © 1975, Fantasy Films and United Artists Corporation)*

MONTANA

SOUTH PARK
613 31ST
BILLINGS, MONTANA

 4/2

970 AM

If there's no run here, take after the name of the town's other good park—Optimist—and be one. Cruise Lillis and Rose parks, which have been known to draw a crowd.

SOUTH GYM
MONTANA STATE UNIVERSITY
BOZEMAN, MONTANA

4/2
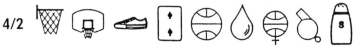
93.7 FM

When Boze-men aren't schussing around, which isn't all that often, they show here. If for some reason there's been a thaw and it's over-crowded, check out one of the five other gyms on campus.

KNIGHTS OF COLUMBUS GYM
PARK AND IDAHO
BUTTE, MONTANA

2/1

95.5 FM

The runs in these parts are far from beauts, but this noontime crowd on weekdays gets the nod over the lunch bunch at the Y. Still, expect upward mobility in the nonhoops sense, only.

HEISEY YOUTH CENTER
313 7TH NORTH
GREAT FALLS, MONTANA

4/2   98.9 FM

Pick-up unfolds here, but leagues are the real thing. There's something for everyone, from an over-thirty loop to a coed league.

YMCA
LYNDALE AND LAST CHANCE GULCH
HELENA, MONTANA

6/3   1340 AM

Where ''shooting the place up at Last Chance Gulch'' means there'll be a ballgame, not a Western.

REC ANNEX
UNIVERSITY OF MONTANA
MISSOULA, MONTANA

4/2   1320 AM

Those who enjoy lofting Js into the big sky will find their prospects hereabouts somewhat grisly. Almost all the rocking takes place in the Annex.

NEBRASKA

MALONE COMMUNITY CENTER
22ND AND T
LINCOLN, NEBRASKA

2/1   102.7 FM

This may not be the most continental of American cities, but it is where the Cadillac run in this town gets garaged. Check it out.

MEN'S P.E. BUILDING
UNIVERSITY OF NEBRASKA
LINCOLN, NEBRASKA

6/3   102.7 FM

Great old-time rec-hall atmosphere here, where the tall stalks grow. Talk about Big Men on Campus . . .

FONTENELLE PARK
FONTENELLE AND AMES
OMAHA, NEBRASKA

 2/1   1560 AM

The game is wild enough to make you suspect that Marlon Perkins is a regular. Here "in your mug" also refers to where the root beer goes across the street at the A&W. Also check out Eppley Boys Club, where Heisman Trophy winner Johnny Rogers has done some running.

116

Lincoln *Barnball decor will always have its place in corn country, even at the University of Nebraska's P.E. building, where husky Huskers run. (David Creamer)*

COUGARS PALACE
NEBRASKA WESTERN JUNIOR COLLEGE
SCOTTSBLUFF, NEBRASKA

6/3  960 AM

This isn't a gambling den, but where many a juco juker has galloped up and down the wood.

NEVADA

REC CENTER
WILLIAM AND ROOP
CARSON CITY, NEVADA

6/3 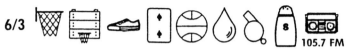 105.7 FM

The action isn't too terribly heavy here. In Carson, ''Doc'' is more likely to refer to Severinsen than Erving.

YOUTH CENTER
107 WEST BASIC
HENDERSON, NEVADA

4/1  102 FM

According to the long-standing rule here, you can pick no more than two players off the losing team. When the local street-gang members have just lost, it would be politic to consider choosing them. More racks outside.

DULA REC CENTER
LAS VEGAS AND BONANZA
LAS VEGAS, NEVADA

2/1  88.1 FM

This is a sort of UNLV alumni house, servicing the many Runnin' Rebel types who still call Vegas their crib and make a living in the casinos, (roulette) wheeling and (card) dealing. When the house is full, you're advised to stay home with anything less than a strong hand.

COMMANDO BASKETBALL

Reno is Springfield, Massachusetts, to the game of Commando Hoops, a whimsical diversion invented on the Nevada-Reno campus. It's hoops with the added fillip that each player wears—and uses—one sixteen-ounce boxing glove.

All basketball rules apply, except:

1. Any player landing a scoring blow to an opponent who possesses the ball is awarded two free throws, unless the sluggee has succeeded in converting a field goal while being struck, in which case the slug-gee gets a well-deserved three foul shots, and a Purple Heart.

2. Any player punched when not in possession of the ball receives two free throws.

The natural tendency to avoid being hit, coupled with the difficulty of grasping a ball while wearing a boxing glove, results in a lot of loose balls.

Playing tip: If you've got the ball and are about to be hit, simply flip it to your would-be assailant. If he catches it, he becomes a target.

BILLINGHURST GYM
PLYMOUTH AND MONROE
RENO, NEVADA

Some of the fundamentals of commando basketball, which was born here, inadvertently make their way into the runs. The regulars share this much with the local casino operators: they prefer "winners out."

ALF SORENSEN COMMUNITY CENTER
BERING AND MCCARRAN
SPARKS, NEVADA

A lot of family-style activities take up time here. But when real comp arrives, the families defer and go for a swim.

NEW HAMPSHIRE

YMCA
WARREN AND NORTH STATE
CONCORD, NEW HAMPSHIRE

6/2  102.3 FM

For a sure-bet game, show up any Monday, Wednesday, or Friday at 12:30. Be prepared, though, to share the gym with racquetball players.

AREA TWO COURTS
UNIVERSITY OF NEW HAMPSHIRE
DURHAM, NEW HAMPSHIRE

8/4  91.3 FM

School's never out at these courts, where play rages 'til dusk every summer day. Six more hoops in the campus Fieldhouse should get you through the winter.

ALUMNI GYM
DARTMOUTH COLLEGE
HANOVER, NEW HAMPSHIRE

6/3 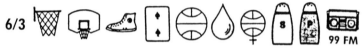 99 FM

Soar physically and mentally in the regular noontime games. The student-faculty ratio is conducive to good education. Lay a little Goethe on Bruce, the German prof, as he wheels into his hook. Or incant some Bhagavad Gita at Amos, who'll relate his Zen basketball theories in return.

Hanover *They don't serve lunch at Alumni Gym until Amos, a fiftyish fixture, shoots for nexts. (Bruce Wood)*

REC CENTER
WASHINGTON AND GILSUM
KEENE, NEW HAMPSHIRE

6/3   103.7 FM

There's an each-one, teach-one philosophy here, where clinics are held four times a year. Underprivileged kids who hang here and behave themselves may be rewarded with free ducats to Keene State games.

121

ASH STREET SCHOOLYARD
MAPLE AND RIDGE
MANCHESTER, NEW HAMPSHIRE

 4/2   1370 AM

The courts have undergone some refurbishing of late, turning what was a legitimate run into an even more solid undertaking. Lights from the nearby intersection shed plenty of rays over the court, so night play is possible.

YMCA
PROSPECT AND HARBOR
NASHUA, NEW HAMPSHIRE

6/3   106.3 FM

With the exception of a church league, organized play is scarce, but that bodes well for pick-up freaks. Best times: lunch hour or after 5:30.

SOUTH PLAYGROUND
SOUTH AND PARROTT
PORTSMOUTH, NEW HAMPSHIRE

 2/1   92.8 FM

The setting: beautiful. The play: excellent—for these parts, at least. See if you can figure out who Teddy Lilakos, the guy they named the league after, is. And try cracking the regulars' run at the JFK Community Center, where the faces never change, and the moves just get slower.

Portsmouth *The Teddy Lilakos clock/ scoreboard/P.A. system gets its juice from a South Playground regular's ride. (Dean Ludington)*

NEW JERSEY

BOYS CLUB
PROSPECT
ASBURY PARK, NEW JERSEY

4/1   1310 AM

Serious fastbreak ball. A fellow from around these parts once said it best—something about being born to run.

WEST SIDE COMPLEX
ILLINOIS
ATLANTIC CITY, NEW JERSEY

 4/2    1490 AM

It's a "complex" because there's an indoor court, too. Hackers will have a better chance at the tables off the Boardwalk.

FARNHAM PARK
PARK AND BAIRD
CAMDEN, NEW JERSEY

 4/2    105.3 FM

"It's a regular war on these courts," says one insider of this spot, in the Parkside section of town, right across from that hoops haven, Camden High. Other hotbeds, by neighborhood, include: Dudley Grange Park (East Camden), Rev. Evers Park (Morgan Village), and Elijah Perry Park (Centerville). As for indoor play, Y not? It's at Third and Federal.

MEMORIAL PARK
LENOLA
CINNAMINSON, NEW JERSEY

  3/1   105.3 FM

The summer league features no foul outs, a three-point shot, and a thirty-second clock. Ergo, pick-up play tends to be rough-and-tumble, and marked by long shots launched frequently.

ST. ROSE SCHOOLYARD
WHITE HORSE PIKE AND KINGS
HADDONFIELD, NEW JERSEY

 2/1    99 FM

''We're basically the 'play-to-sixteen-switch-at-eight-to-get-an-even-tan crowd,' '' says one vet of this spot, where action begins stirring 3ish on summer afternoons. One con: the court is tilted a bit. One pro: Del's Deli is nearby.

ST. JOSEPH'S SCHOOLYARD
511 PAVONIA
JERSEY CITY, NEW JERSEY

 6/3      95 FM

You'll find every race and creed, with the main run at center court. Summers, it's not uncommon to find some of Jersey's best white hopes. Mike O'Koren and Jim Spanarkel came up on these slabs.

COMMUNITY CENTER
PRINCETON AND MONMOUTH
LAKEWOOD, NEW JERSEY

 2/1      1170 AM

The shake-and-bake is so good that the summer league here attracts local cable coverage. The milkshake-and-cheesesteak isn't bad, either— courtesy vendor Mr. Jay. The court was a $54,000 project, about which this community is justifiably proud.

THE HEADLINER COURT
ROUTE 35 SOUTH AND NEW YORK
NEPTUNE, NEW JERSEY

  2/1   107.5 FM

Have a pop or two at the Headliner, then watch folks like Kelly Tripucka and Mike O'Koren pop a few outside this Jersey Shore bar. The summer league here is an annual ritual for many, and the bleachers by the fenced-in court offer plenty of seating.

YMCA
600 BROAD
NEWARK, NEW JERSEY

6/3   ...   88.3 FM

The pick-up is good, but the house team—a recent AAU/Junior Olympic national champ—keeps pride high and the trophy case stocked. Recommended tuneage is the jazz of WBGO, Radio Free Newark.

6TH STREET COURTS
6TH AND OCEANFRONT
OCEAN CITY, NEW JERSEY

 6/3   95.1 FM

Back when all the Irish Catholic kids were wearing their St. Christopher medals, summer hoops in O City was big doings. The local league, under the guidance of ACC ref Hank Armstrong, is as strong as ever, and has given pick-up play new life as well.

REC CENTER
RIVER AND CHESTNUT
POINT PLEASANT, NEW JERSEY

 2/1    107.1 FM

Dunk, and you'll be assessed for damages. Ask Dominic, the director, about the game he invented called "Pressure 21." If it rains, he'll let you inside the gym.

COMMUNITY PARK SCHOOLYARD
JOHN AND BIRCH
PRINCETON, NEW JERSEY

 101.5 FM

Attracts students, townies, and the occasional interloper up from Trenton. Indoors, there's Dillon and Jadwin gyms on campus, both with worthwhile noontime runs. For indulging that midnight urge, there's the Theological Seminary Gym. For years, a group of regulars has gained entry through the second window from the left facing Stockton.

SEA GIRT ELEMENTARY SCHOOLYARD
BELL AND CRESCENT
SEA GIRT, NEW JERSEY

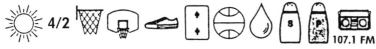 107.1 FM

Players begin materializing around 5 on weekdays, and 1 on weekends, during the summer. The Headliner is just down the road a piece.

Ocean City *It may be a dry town, but that doesn't bar the nightlife from the 6th Street Courts. (Hank Armstrong)*

SKYVIEW PARK
BAY AND VAUGHN
TOMS RIVER, NEW JERSEY

The Ocean County Summer League tips off here. It's one of the East's best-run and best-refereed loops. The zebras take home twenty bucks a game.

CADWALADER PLAYGROUND
PARKSIDE AND WEST STATE
TRENTON, NEW JERSEY

We imagine you've already O.D.'d on the cold hot dogs and warm sodas, and shot your wad on side bets. So, while waiting on a run here, we suggest you ponder this: What does the civic slogan, "Trenton Makes, the World Takes," mean in hoopspeak?

SUFFOLK AVENUE COURT
SUFFOLK AND BOARDWALK
VENTNOR, NEW JERSEY

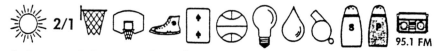

Quintessential Jersey Shore hoopage. Postgame, go to the Boardwalk— do not pass GO—and chill out in the ocean. Former 'Nova and NBA guard Chris Ford had his day here.

If Al McGuire thinks it's tough to play without an aircraft carrier, he should try playing on one. (Pat Millea)

THE BASE LINE

If you're not quite up to swapping a few years of your life just to get in some good ball, panic not. In most cases, you can get "down" for a game on a military base without enlisting for more than just a run. (It's tougher to get a run on the U.S.S. *Tripoli,* where someone will yell, "Steel Beach!" and a hoop will suddenly appear in the hangar bay.) Getting into gyms is easy once you've gotten on the base itself; to do *that,* sometimes a buddy with a base-access sticker on his car has to do. But, once there, you'll find the taxpayer-underwritten facilities first-rate, and the style a fine cross-section of bro-inspired innovation and hick-inspired fundamentals. As one Navy man in the know tells us, "Command-directed awareness of equal-opportunity goals prevents some of the subtle lockouts that can occur on 'black' and 'white' courts." At ease.

NEW MEXICO

WELLS PARK COMMUNITY CENTER
5TH AND MOUNTAIN
ALBUQUERQUE, NEW MEXICO

 6/3 ... 1520 AM

If you're A-Team and in A-Town, here's where you'll want to strut your stuffs. A scenic run that's a notch lower competitively can be found at Trumbull Park. Other spots: the Dennis Chavez and Heights community centers.

FORT CANYON PARK
FORD
GALLUP, NEW MEXICO

 4/2 ... 1330 AM

If you were to canvass these courts, you'd find "nineteen different nationalities," according to an insider. Salt, pepper, jalapeño pepper.

WASHINGTON PARK
MARLAND AND 5TH
HOBBS, NEW MEXICO

 2/1   102 FM

There's a reason the local high school holds the national prep record for the highest scoring average in a season (114.6 a game, 1970), and this spot has a lot to do with it. They run, they gun, they full-court press.

*And they've banned zones from the summer league up at Tasker Arena.
"Play one," says Doug, the supe, "and it's an automatic T, just like
in the NBA."*

MILES PARK
CAMINO CARLOS REY AND SIRINGO
SANTA FE, NEW MEXICO

 6/3
106.1 FM

*This is a city that prides itself on being hip. Fortunately, the hip-hop-
pers out here keep things in proper perspective. A lot of Carloses and
gringos, as well as bros, make their way to Carlos Rey and Siringo.
Indoors, they run out of the Fort Marcy Complex.*

NEW YORK

THE CITY

East Side, West Side, all around the town they play the game—differently, to be sure, from borough to borough. "Ours is a little more laid-back, move the ball around," says one Manhattanite. "In Brooklyn, it's more run 'n' gun." You can take it to the bank, however, that ball anywhere in the Apple involves taking it to the rack. That's as much an imperative of the facilities as the result of the social fabric. No nets means no sweet outside jump shooters. No space means no "clearing" of the ball beyond the foul line. "New York City style is different from any other kind of style," says the Bronx's own Walter (The Truth) Berry. "Hey, most of the guys six-eight—my size—can bring the ball up." So, what *do* you call a burg that not only has a court, in Brooklyn, known as The Hole, but a *tournament* there, too, called Soul in the Hole? King of the hill, top of the heap.

THE VALLEY
HAMMERSLEY AND GUNTHER
BRONX, NEW YORK

 6/3  107.5 FM

Not to be confused with The Hole, which is in Brooklyn. A P.B.C. (predominantly black crowd) welcomes white dudes who can play. Switch hoops at "halftime," which is halfway to forty by twos, and look for Mt. Vernonites who make the journey down from Westchester because of this spot's rep.

THE HOLE
MONROE AND SUMNER
BROOKLYN, NEW YORK

 2/1  98.7 FM

Quiz time. Why's this spot, known to the more straitlaced as P.S. 44 Schoolyard, called The Hole? Because it's below street level? "Not too imaginative, but very precise," says Dudley, who runs the Soul in the Hole league here on summer Saturdays, from 10 " 'til." He says there's never been a Soul in the Hole game played with naked holes, "but keeping those nets up—that's the struggle."

MANHATTAN BEACH PARK
ORIENTAL
BROOKLYN, NEW YORK

 6/3    **92 FM**

Summer weekend runs are a ritual here. The lore, on the other hand, is tough to sort out. We've heard that this is where Billy C. came up, and where Brooklyn's best-looking women do their bathing.

ST. JOHN'S REC CENTER
PROSPECT AND SCHENECTADY
BROOKLYN, NEW YORK

 6/3      **107.5 FM**

Best runs are weekend mornings; Tuesday nights are officially designated "Ladies Nights," when women only can play. Not much of an outdoor scene here anymore, so cruise Foster ("Heaven," where twelve racks can be found) or Kingston (where the shaded court is reserved for the women) parks, or the Brevoort Projects, a.k.a. The Brooklyn Coliseum.

MARTIN LUTHER KING PARK
BEST AND HUMBOLDT
BUFFALO, NEW YORK

 4/2   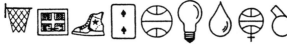   **94 FM**

The main court can accommodate 3,600 for a Randy Smith summer league game. Check out the patter and chatter of P.A. man Willie Earl House. Check out the Stone City All-Stars, Rick James's team and a perennial league power. And check out their number-1 fan, squeaky-clean rocker Donny Osmond, who has—would we lie to you?—sat on their bench. Action is nearly as good at the three slabs over at Delaware Park.

Buffalo *Only a galvanizing force like King Park's Smith League could bring Donny Osmond and Rick James together. (Michael Baugh)*

MOFFETT GYM
CORTLAND STATE UNIVERSITY
CORTLAND, NEW YORK

6/3
920 AM

A good crowd can be counted on here, where you'll be treated to that rarity, a parquet floor. Lose, and you could wait an hour for another crack.

PROSPECT PARK
PROSPECT
EAST MEADOW, NEW YORK

 6/3
107.5 FM

With such good comp and good courts, it's a shame the lights go out at 10. One rule to abide by: never go baseline on someone whose name ends in stein *or* berg.

134

QUEENSBURY RACQUET CLUB
91 GLENWOOD
GLENS FALLS, NEW YORK

   4/2   106 FM

An indoor tennis facility that has caught on to the hoops boom. Several hundred players pay $3 a week for their fix, plus towel service, showers and saunas, and a lounge.

SUMMER'S RESORT
DUNE
HAMPTON BAYS, NEW YORK

 2/1    107.1 FM

Sun, suds, and hoops all go together at this beachfront club. Summer weekends find the court—and the courtside bar—full of partying yups.

CAMPBELL PARK
LINDEN AND PENINSULA
HEMPSTEAD, NEW YORK

 6/3    98.7 FM

The sign at Roosevelt Park would lead you to believe otherwise, but the Doc played here first—until ninth grade. (He used to live across the street.) Games are played "straight five" to twenty-one: if both teams have twenty, the first team to score five times wins.

BARTON HALL
CORNELL UNIVERSITY
ITHACA, NEW YORK

12/6    91.7 FM

Most of the time this place looks like a three-ring circus: karate classes here, baton twirling there, and hoops taking center stage. Barton is so vast that it's a cinch to lose yourself inside after hours for a midnight run.

COLUMBUS PARK
VAN RANST AND MAMARONECK
MAMARONECK, NEW YORK

 3/1   107.5 FM

Play at night? Flip that switch. Play seriously? *Join the Twilight League. Eat pizza? Slide up the street. Mikeman David has become a Twilight League fixture. Look for J-up Jay Twyman, Jack's son.*

THE ASPHALT GREEN
92ND AND YORK
MANHATTAN, NEW YORK

 4/2   107.5 FM

So named because someone put a verdant paintbrush to the backboards. A drainage gulch just to the left of one lane will put you out of commission if you're not careful. Dogs, meanwhile, can be dispatched to the ASPCA, which is just a block or two uptown.

HOLCOMBE RUCKER PLAYGROUND
155TH AND EIGHTH
MANHATTAN, NEW YORK

 2/1    98.7 FM

"The Battleground" of legend and lore. While the Rucker Tournament has moved indoors, this seminal playground has recently hosted something called the Remy City Game Challenge, matching pick-up teams from some of the hoopiest cities around the land. Winners copped such streetwise prizes as . . . a trip to France. En votre visage.

P.S. 175 SCHOOLYARD
135TH AND LENOX
MANHATTAN, NEW YORK

 1/0   98.7 FM

This single court is newly resealed and had a cameo role in John Sayles's movie Brother from Another Planet. *The backboard is wood, a New York rarity. Right next door is the 135th Street Y.*

Manhattan *If you don't agree with this boast at P.S. 175 Schoolyard, come on up—and put on up or shut on up.*

Manhattan *The ladies meet above the street in Cecil King's distaff league at P.S. 134 Park. (Magda Santos)*

P.S. 134 PARK
HENRY AND EAST BROADWAY
MANHATTAN, NEW YORK

Of the three sites around town where Cecil King runs his women's summer league, this attracts the most people and generates the best atmosphere. It's rough, says Cecil; ''the court is so small, and we've got some big women.''

RIVERSIDE PARK
102ND AND RIVERSIDE
MANHATTAN, NEW YORK

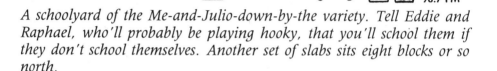

A schoolyard of the Me-and-Julio-down-by-the variety. Tell Eddie and Raphael, who'll probably be playing hooky, that you'll school them if they don't school themselves. Another set of slabs sits eight blocks or so north.

THE BALLOT OF CONNIE & HIS GLIDE

During their day, New York City playground legends and NBA coulda-beens like Earl Manigault, Joe Hammond, and Herman (Helicopter) Knowings stirred spectators and impressed peers. But for all their back-alley pyrotechnics, none could match the sheer rep of a sho'nuff-was named Connie Hawkins. During one Sixties summer The Hawk failed to show for a single Rucker League game. Still, the coaches voted him to the All-Star Team. As ex-Rucker honcho Bob McCullough told Pete Axthelm in *The City Game*: "If you're going to have an all-star game in Harlem, you vote for Connie or you don't vote." The Hawk *did* show for the game—and swooped off with the MVP award.

STUYVESANT TOWN COURTS
18TH and FIRST
MANHATTAN, NEW YORK

This is as fundamentally sound a run as you'll find in the city, sort of open-air Catholic Youth Organization–style, occasionally spiced up with

cameos by Dean Meminger and Dick Barnett, who live in the project. Switch hoops at midgame, because of the uneven heights of the rims. Summers, late afternoon, there's a regular run.

VANDERBILT YMCA
47TH AND SECOND
MANHATTAN, NEW YORK

2/1   **107.5 FM**

The zestiest middle-aged full-court run in town unleashes the full fury of its many midlife crises on Tuesday and Thursday mornings. Be kind to the guy from Holland wearing black socks who stumbled into a game and doesn't have a clue; the building is a sort of youth hostel for international backpackers. Among other Apple Ys, West Side has the best facilities; McBurney the earliest run (6:30 a.m.); and Inwood the finest league.

WEST 4TH STREET PLAYGROUND
WEST 4TH AND SIXTH
MANHATTAN, NEW YORK

 3/1      **98.7 FM**

There may be no court in the country with more urban ambience and flat-out streetwise style than this one, right smack in Greenwich Village. A concessionaire in Moslem dress sells potions, incense, and copies of the Koran. Ken Graham, the summer league commissioner, uses the trunk of his taxicab as an office. Check out Slinky, the guy from the Bronx with the moves.

THE VILLAGE VOICE

Omar Khayyam works the scoreboard at the West 4th Street Summer Pro Classic in New York City. For more than a decade, he's drifted down from his room in a midtown Manhattan transient hotel to the city's *al fresco* hoops hall of fame in Greenwich Village, where he wields a mean piece of chalk.

Omar is also a talking book of park lore. He can tell you how a local restaurateur led a campaign a few years ago to tear down the court and replace it with a "sculpture park." How the regulars angrily reacted, turning West 4th Street's preservation into a *cause célèbre*. And how,

So long as Omar's around, the electric scoreboard at West 4th Street will never blow a fuse. (Paul Bereswill)

ultimately, the Parks Department struck a deal with summer league commissioner Ken Graham to keep the facilities spic 'n' span. The resulting improvements stripped West 4th of some of the untidiness from which it got its charm. But that much-needed dose of civilization has left many others satisfied, perhaps even that hostile restaurateur. As the league rumbles into its second decade, Khayyam still stands courtside, where he runs what Graham calls "our electric scoreboard."

"Omar was born in Brooklyn and raised in Newark," the commish says. "He'll die on West Fourth Street."

SMITH CLOVE PARK
SPRING
MONROE, NEW YORK

A trio of slabs, well lit and well maintained. A quality summer league attracts a good crowd that comes back for pick-up play.

BASKETBALL CENTER
WEST 4TH AND SEVENTH
MT. VERNON, NEW YORK

A bro's bro facility. Among the ones you'll find are Gus Williams's Ray, and Rodney McCray's Scooter. And the name doesn't pull any punches.

BOYS CLUB
LINCOLN
NEW ROCHELLE, NEW YORK

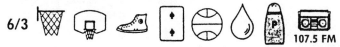

And on the seventh day, you come here. Slip in the back door and get your handle on the ever-lengthening list of who's ''down.'' No time for Sunday brunch? A local entrepreneur has donuts and beverages he'll deal you in on for some up-front scratch. Sorry, no credit.

CENTER COURT COMMUNITY CENTER
CENTER
NIAGARA FALLS, NEW YORK

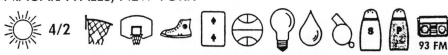

Great name, huh? Home to the Frank Layden Summer League. There's a full court inside.

141

SHEA'S BARN
724 PICKERING
OGDENSBURG, NEW YORK

2/1    96 FM

Barnball finds its niche in a converted hayloft near the Canadian border. The springtime three-on-three is particularly rough, and is made more so by the 9'5'' rims.

Ogdensburg *The phrase ''hit the boards'' takes on a whole new meaning at Shea's, where you're really hurting if you can't hit the broad side of a barn. (Dave Shea)*

BORDMANVILLE PARK
1ST AND NORTH UNION
OLEAN, NEW YORK

 2/1   101 FM

In this neck of the woods—and we do mean woods—you take your games where you can.

HULME PARK
CHURCH AND MARKET
POUGHKEEPSIE, NEW YORK

 2/1   .98 FM

The shaking-and-baking takes place in the Unity Summer League. The moving-and-shaking is director Bakari Adeyemi's. The league is a little loose, but no director can claim a better handle.

FATHER GROGAN MEMORIAL PLAYGROUND
129TH AND ROCKAWAY BEACH
QUEENS, NEW YORK

 6/3   98.7 FM

With the church on one side and the beach on the other, there's little that beats the St. Francis de Sales Summer Classic, which is played here. The court has recently been resurfaced. This is the parish that brought you the McGuire brothers; look for Al's nieces. They aren't exactly aircraft carriers, but pretty fair players themselves.

MONTEBELLIER PLAYGROUND
138TH AND SPRINGFIELD
QUEENS, NEW YORK

 6/3   98.7 FM

One of the sites of the venerable Elmcor Neighborhood League. For pick-up play, one court is designated "Half-Court Only." Also, check out Elmcor's alternative site, the recently renovated P.S. 127 Schoolyard in East Elmhurst.

COBBS HILL PARK
MONROE AND CULVER
ROCHESTER, NEW YORK

 2/1   103.9 FM

Some refurbishing is going on at this spot, which sits right smack twixt city and suburb, thus attracting a variegated clientele. Another pair of racks is supposed to go up when the funding comes down.

KIDERA GYM
NAZARETH COLLEGE
ROCHESTER, NEW YORK

6/3   103.9 FM

Honest: You've got to be on the "guest list" to get in this gym. Most of the names, like J.J. White's, already "registered" are major-college, semipro, and pro types. But more power to you if you can get on—and in.

HICKEY FIELD
SUNRISE
ROCKVILLE CENTRE, NEW YORK

 6/3      101 FM

The comp has tailed off in recent years, but the summer-league triple-headers on each of these three courts still draw hoop groupies.

CENTENNIAL PARK
CENTENNIAL AND BABYLON
ROOSEVELT, NEW YORK

 16/8      98.7 FM

Could be Long Island's finest run. Why does the comp come here, rather than to Roosevelt Park, where (as the sign says) "Julius Erving learned the game of basketball"? Shrugs Willie, the summer-league director: "We're right on the bus line."

144

EAST SIDE REC FIELD
LAKE
SARATOGA SPRINGS, NEW YORK

 6/3

Thoroughbreds race here every summer evening, only a few furlongs from the storied racetrack.

SUNNYCREST PARK
ROBINSON AND TEALL
SYRACUSE, NEW YORK

 8/4

Those who have nexts will encounter no day-in-the-park here, where you can often color those who show (Syracuse U.) Orange.

WILSON PARK
MCBRIDE AND JACKSON
SYRACUSE, NEW YORK

 6/3

A good run, even if it's in a housing project with the dubious name of Brick City. Recently resurfaced, with a summer tournament that has attracted some attention. Also check out Barry Park, where Dolph Schayes once played.

PROSPECT PARK
PAWLING
TROY, NEW YORK

 4/2

The battles of Troy are waged here every day. If you're a white dude who shoots an airball, the bros charitably assume it was meant to be an alley-oop.

NORTH CAROLINA

REID REC CENTER
LIVINGSTON AND CHOCTAW
ASHEVILLE, NORTH CAROLINA

6/3   99.9 FM

Madness in the mountains, especially during the summer. Reid's solid rep is the work of such well-Heeled regulars as Buzz Peterson and Brad Daugherty.

GRANVILLE TOWERS COURT
UNIVERSITY OF NORTH CAROLINA
CHAPEL HILL, NORTH CAROLINA

 2/1      107 FM

Stereos, sunbathers, and an abundance of other collegiate diversions are nearby. Features a tarred heel at center court, as if it were the campus' Carmichael Auditorium (which, by the way, has some great summer runs).

HARGRAVES PARK
WEST ROSEMARY AND ROBERSON
CHAPEL HILL, NORTH CAROLINA

 8/4      107 FM

The lights blaze 'til 10 in winter, an hour or so later during the summer. Check out the gym at the old Lincoln High, which the city leases for free play and league play.

AMAY JAMES REC CENTER
2425 LESTER
CHARLOTTE, NORTH CAROLINA

4/2   1600 AM

Things are usually interesting here, especially when Walter Davis and Cornbread Maxwell come 'round. There's a super summer league, too (the best winter leaguers rap at Sugar Hill Rec Center). If you have a red, white, and blue getup, check out Freedom and Independence parks.

POWER LUNCHES

To eat or not to eat, that is the question. Whether 'tis wiser to catch a quick bite before heading for the gym (at the risk of cramps or sluggishness), or to hold off (at the risk of anemia) in accordance with that adage about a hungry dog hunting best. . . . Every type, from Shakespearean scholars to school janitors, has faced that dilemma some weekday around 11:30 A.M. That's about when games get underway at countless college gyms around the country, where noontime hoops can be as hallowed an institution as Old Siwash itself.

At Brigham Young, faculty and staff have the right to bump any student between noon and 1 P.M. At Navy, the regulars hew to the 85-

These regulars at UNC-Greensboro's Coleman Gym—a typical college lunch bunch—aren't looking for a handout, just a Coleman stove.

147

degree rule: if the temperature is above 85, the skins are considered to be at an advantage, so the shirts get first outs; below 85, it's vice versa. The heating at North Carolina–Greensboro's Coleman Gym is erratic, so winter games aren't run shirts 'n' skins, but practically sweatshirts 'n' parkas. Across town, the Guilford College lunch bunch calls its thrice-weekly noontime sessions "committee meetings," the better to get out of any conflicting commitments that arise. And beware the three-on-three at Princeton's Jadwin Gym, where coach Pete Carril can put his antiquated set-shot—along with his stogie—in your face.

Similar diurnal rituals are enacted at countless Ys and municipal rec centers, too. You undress on the run, forego warm-ups, play, and hustle back to work. Hey, there isn't any *time* to eat.

So long as heaven is a playground, does it matter? You get your manna from heaven.

MORREENE ROAD PARK
MORREENE AND SHERWOOD
DURHAM, NORTH CAROLINA

 4/2

Best runs are on the weekends, when lots of Dukies make the short trek over. Lights are controlled by the participants, so play sometimes goes '' 'til.''

WEST DURHAM PARK
HILLSBOROUGH AND HILLANDALE
DURHAM, NORTH CAROLINA

 4/2

The crowd tends to be of the weekend and lunch-hour variety. A fetching setting, with the city reservoir in the background. Lyon Park is a bit harder to find (take Lakewood to Cornell), but just as pretty.

J.S. SPIVEY PROJECT GYM
FISHER
FAYETTEVILLE, NORTH CAROLINA

6/3

The only free gym in town. You'll also find two hoops outdoors. Just a notch behind Rocky Mount's Booker T for hoops supremacy in eastern Carolina.

ERWIN CENTER
913 NORTH PRYOR
GASTONIA, NORTH CAROLINA

6/3   97.9 FM

On that august occasion—or was it in April?—when two Erwin products, Sleepy Floyd and James Worthy, hooked up in the NCAA title game, CBS featured a spot on this spot at halftime. The segment focused on how Georgetown and Carolina had each found a star in the same firmament.

DOUGLAS PARK
DOUGLAS
GREENSBORO, NORTH CAROLINA

 2/1     90.1 FM

The young Danny Manning spent a good bit of time here, and Bob McAdoo still swings by occasionally. 'Adoo run-runs over at Windsor Rec Center, too.

LAKE DANIEL PARK
EAST LAKE
GREENSBORO, NORTH CAROLINA

 2/1    90.1 FM

A quintessential suburban park, where professionals (doctors and lawyers, not NBAers and CBAers) abound. The racks always have nets, but if you want to play volleyball, you'd better bring your own.

ELM STREET GYM
ELM AND 14TH
GREENVILLE, NORTH CAROLINA

6/3   97 FM

The tile floor may take some getting used to, but it does provide the best squeak in the South. Weather permitting, check out the two outdoor courts around the corner on 14th, hard by the East Carolina freshman dorms.

RIDGEVIEW REC CENTER
FIRST
HICKORY, NORTH CAROLINA

4/2
1290 AM

From Walter Davis and David Thompson to John Drew and Chris Washburn, a bunch of studfish spent their Wonder years here. Some nights the runs are simply awesome.

CENTRAL FAMILY YMCA
150 HARTLEY
HIGH POINT, NORTH CAROLINA

6/3
97 FM

Put your initials on the blackboard to get in a game here, where comp can be found seven days a week, except during the furniture mart held each April and October. If you don't have an ex-collegian or current schoolboy stud in your house, expect to sit after one run.

SOUTHEAST PARK
TIFFANY AND BRIGHT
KINSTON, NORTH CAROLINA

 6/3
97 FM

How you approach this spot is as important as how you play once there. We advise: (1) park your car in the elementary school lot; (2) call "nexts," and bide your time perched atop your car hood; and (3) hold court as long as you can. Afterward, adjourn to Rayner's for refreshments—or (why not?) to Hallowell Community Center for more ball.

STANLEY WHITE REC CENTER
CHAPMAN AND CEDAR
NEW BERN, NORTH CAROLINA

2/1
97 FM

Aside from warm-up games of "21," play here is almost exclusively full court. Best dishin' is done on Tuesday and Thursday nights, and Saturdays 10 'til 2.

CARMICHAEL COURTS
NORTH CAROLINA STATE UNIVERSITY
RALEIGH, NORTH CAROLINA

 4/2   89.9 FM

The courts are oversized, so play is strictly half court. Lots of townies crash the action. The more serious go indoors to the adjacent Phys Ed building. Sneaking in's a snap: just don red gym shorts and a gray T-shirt, give the student guard a wave, and cruise.

MILLBROOK EXCHANGE REC CENTER
SPRING FOREST
RALEIGH, NORTH CAROLINA

6/3   88.9 FM

Get on the sign-up sheet. House rules say games go to ten, but they usually run to sixteen by common consent. You won't see Dean Smith prowling the sidelines for recruits. Otherwise, service can be had from Kiwanis and Lions parks. At the former, when the illumination gets ill-tempered, players pull their cars up on the grass and run their head-lights off the battery so they can light it up. At the latter, you'll want to stay friendly with Dennis, a motorcycle gang member who hangs out.

Kinston *At Southeast Park you're going against the grain if you're not an elevator man.*

BOOKER T. WASHINGTON GYM
CAROLINA
ROCKY MOUNT, NORTH CAROLINA

6/3   1490 AM

This spot's rep was undeservedly tainted among Heel followers when homeboy Phil Ford hurt himself here, playing ball over a Christmas break in the mid-'70s. Baseball Hall of Famer Buck Leonard used to work here, and lives nearby.

MARTIN LUTHER KING CENTER
401 SOUTH 8TH
WILMINGTON, NORTH CAROLINA

4/2   1390 AM

This is your garden-variety MLK, business as usual. Hellacious hoops, once home to Michael Jordan.

HANES HOSIERY REC CENTER
501 REYNOLDS
WINSTON-SALEM, NORTH CAROLINA

6/3   980 AM

Built by the nylons folks, and—unlike their products—prone to big-time runs. See if inspector No. 12 doesn't have a sweet J. For outdoor play, Happy Hill Park offers two racks.

NORTH DAKOTA

WORLD WAR MEMORIAL CENTER
215 NORTH 6TH
BISMARCK, NORTH DAKOTA

2/1

Heaviest traffic during the noon hour, for what the rec director describes as ''the Businessman's Special.'' Games are played sans musique.

JERRY SCHERLING COURT COMPLEX
302 SOUTH 7TH
FARGO, NORTH DAKOTA

  4/2

A brand-new hoops-and-tennis complex, with a 700-seat amphitheater for big summer-league tilts.

YMCA FAMILY CENTER
7TH AND UNIVERSITY
GRAND FORKS, NORTH DAKOTA

6/2

It's so chilly here—''the coldest noontime game in the nation,'' the director says—that center jumps take place in what's called the Arctic Circle.

NECTAR OF THE GODS

We've heard all the arguments for beer (carbo loading!), and the familiar neighborhood spot (why cease to hang just 'cause it's *après* ball?), and ice-cold H_2O (which nine out of ten doctors recommend). But in mid-July, nothing—*nothing*—beats cooling down your hot hand by wrapping it around a Chilly Willy.

A Chilly Willy is kind of like a Slurpee, only tangier and icier. It's kind of like a Slush Puppy, only smoother.

And if it doesn't give you a headache, you're either not drinking it fast enough, or weren't playing hard enough.

MEMORIAL GYM
JAMESTOWN COLLEGE
JAMESTOWN, NORTH DAKOTA

4/2
1400 AM

Like the buffalo that once roamed these parts, twenty-four-hour gyms are almost extinct. But here's one. We have it on good authority that the fountain provides the coolest and tastiest water in the state.

MUNICIPAL AUDITORIUM
420 3RD
MINOT, NORTH DAKOTA

2/1
92.9 FM

This spot is center court for a winter league servicing 100-plus teams. Summers, league play is strictly three-on-three.

OHIO

PERKINS WOODS PARK
730 PERKINS
AKRON, OHIO

 6/3      108 FM

For those who want to gusjohnson Gus Johnson, bring your game here, where the former NBA hangman still plays. Check out the pool on the hill—as the Beatles might say—for postgame therapy. There's also a good game at the University of Akron's Memorial Hall.

BEACHWOOD COURTS
27000 RICHMOND
BEACHWOOD, OHIO

 6/3      107.9 FM

Michael, the local hoops maven, holds court with tips and tales from noon to 2 on most summer days. He's a fond fixture whose Beachwood-aged rap is becoming legendary.

URBAN LEAGUE COMMUNITY CENTER
SHERRICK AND 13TH
CANTON, OHIO

10/5      106.9 FM

You won't want to miss this run, in a new facility that attracts the area's best. If you yearn for the out-of-doors, Nimisilla Park awaits.

CENTRAL PARKWAY YMCA
CENTRAL AND ELM
CINCINNATI, OHIO

6/3   1480 AM

If more than five are waiting, winners must defer. Plenty of candidates await an opening during the regular Monday night games; forget Wednesdays, when volleyball reigns. Watch out for the Big O himself, a lunchtime occasional.

HARTWELL PARK
GALBRAITH AND VINE
CINCINNATI, OHIO

 4/2      102 FM

The intersection is busy, so watch out when the ball clears the fence. Would-be players cruise the park in their cars; have-been players cruise the pool. Xavier's Schmidt Fieldhouse harbors a no-dirty-stuff summer run.

Cincinnati *Airborne adolescents won't hesitate going over your back at Over-the-Rhine.*

OVER-THE-RHINE COMMUNITY CENTER
GREEN AND REPUBLIC
CINCINNATI, OHIO

6/3    **1480 AM**

A lively evening scene that has the feeling of a high-school party. Regular raps courtesy Alphonso, whose nom de disque *is Hollywood.*

SALVATION ARMY MULTI-PURPOSE COURT
50TH AND HOUGH
CLEVELAND, OHIO

2/1   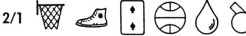   **107.9 FM**

The dude who carries the biggest rep around here is Aparicio Curry. (He, along with Crosetti Speight, Michael Jordan, and several others, is the answer to the arcane trivia question, ''What former college hoopsters have major-league shortstops' last names for first names?'')

WOODLING GYM
CLEVELAND STATE UNIVERSITY
CLEVELAND, OHIO

6/3      **107.9 FM**

One of the best runs in northeast Ohio, especially in the summertime, when it becomes a get-in-shape mecca. Troublemakers are quickly run off by security guards, some of whom play, too.

SCHILLER REC CENTER
CITY PARK AND EAST DESCHLER
COLUMBUS, OHIO

6/3      **92.3 FM**

Ach du Lieber! *This spot, part of a restored German village, offers a single outdoor court, too. See if they're biting in the adjacent pond.*

ROOSEVELT REC CENTER
3RD AND ORCHARD
DAYTON, OHIO

6/3   107.7 FM

This spot has been a fixture for many terms. Double-check your credentials on Tuesdays and Thursdays, when the serious—Jim Paxson, Dwight Anderson, and Herb Williams—bump all mortals off the wood. The summer league at the university's fieldhouse—affectionately called The Pit—is anything but the pits.

BOOKER T. WASHINGTON COMMUNITY CENTER
SOUTH FRONT AND KNIGHTSBRIDGE
HAMILTON, OHIO

2/1   103.5 FM

As Booker T. himself would say, you shoot at buckets where they are, and this isn't exactly settling for second best. Kevin Grevey is the home-grown homeboy, but even Gale Sayers has been known to show.

STRONGSVILLE REC CENTER
ROUTE 82 AND PEARL
STRONGSVILLE, OHIO

 8/4   101.7 FM

Play is steady between 5 and 11 on summer nights. Are you up for the challenge of taking on ''The 'Ville,'' a group of regulars who have played together every Sunday and Wednesday for more than a decade?

CITY PARK
NEBRASKA
TOLEDO, OHIO

 4/2   104.7 FM

There've been happy days here lately, especially since a fellow called The Fonz started running the summer league. A former NBA journeyman named Steve mixes it up on occasion. Check out Westminster Gym, a.k.a. The Catholic Club, as an indoor alternative.

YMCA
HIGH
WARREN, OHIO

4/2

A lot of ex-college and high school jocks. A good dollop of industrial workers keeps the work ethic well represented.

BUCKEYE BUCKS FOR EYES

In many ways, Roger Moll is a redoubtable midwestern burgher. He puts in an honest day's work at the First Buckeye Bank, and scours north central Ohio for ways that his Kiwanis Club can contribute to the greater public good. And so it was that Moll, an upstanding citizen of Willard (pop. 5,720), perfected the concept of civic-mindedness by launching the Willard Kiwanis Hoopfest-Shootout, a three-on-three charity fund-raiser that dribbles up and down the main streets of town.

Since 1984 the Hoopfest-Shootout has raised money through entry fees and the sale of ads. The booty has gone to the handicapped and those who need eyeglasses but can't afford them. Of course, the Hoopfesters themselves are quite hale and possess fairly keen vision,

Willard's ratballers become road warriors in late June of each year. (Jerry Dudek)

159

what with the town's great high-school hoops tradition. (Willard High won sixty-nine regular-season games in a row during the late '70s and early '80s, and the joke is that you have to read the obituary column if you want to get your hands on a Crimson Flashes season ticket.) They save the last Thursday, Friday, and Saturday in June to fill up Myrtle and Pearl streets, "just," Moll says, "like a carnival."

You might even say that the Hoopfest-Shootout is *the* summer event in Willard. Says one local, "*Anything* would be *the* summer event in Willard."

MUNICIPAL PARK
561 WEST LAUREL
WILLARD, OHIO

 4/2 102.7 FM

This is the place to run when the Willard Kiwanis Hoopfest-Shootout isn't happening. Recently refurbished, with comp more intense than that at the three "neighborhood" courts around town.

COMMUNITY CENTER
360 HIGHLAND
WORTHINGTON, OHIO

8/4 880 AM

Serious players in the capital city say "Goodbye, Columbus" and make the short trek over here, especially for the summer loop. One court has a wood floor, the other a carpeted one. Best of all, there's a 1,200-amp stereo system for serious jamming.

HILLMAN PLAYGROUND
HILLMAN AND FALLS
YOUNGSTOWN, OHIO

 6/3 1500 AM

Youngstown State players regularly come by, as does John Bagley. Crandall Park also draws an earnest run, while high schoolers comprise the Mill Creek Community Center's clientele.

OKLAHOMA

PERCEFULL FIELDHOUSE
NORTHWESTERN OKLAHOMA STATE UNIVERSITY
ALVA, OKLAHOMA

6/3

Visitors are welcome in the noontime games that rage every weekday. Lunch-bunch regulars like to boast about their victory over a Dallas Cowboys' squad led by Drew Pearson. Then again, in Oklahoma, any victory over any Texans gets crowed about.

WILL ROGERS ELEMENTARY SCHOOLYARD
1215 EAST 9TH
EDMOND, OKLAHOMA

4/2

The racks are so low that they pretty much render moot what Will Rogers himself once said: ''We can't all be heroes because someone has to sit on the curb and clap as they go by.''

ENID GARFIELD YMCA
WEST CHEROKEE AND ADAMS
ENID, OKLAHOMA

4/2

This is Mark Price's hometown, though playing here isn't a pricey proposition. The largest indoor court in town has ample room around the wood, and throws its doors open to anyone.

COMMUNITY CENTER
301 SOUTH HOWARD
MOORE, OKLAHOMA

6/3      100 FM

A clean, well-lighted place, with everything in order: the balls, the floor, the AC.

REC CENTER
CALLAHAN AND C
MUSKOGEE, OKLAHOMA

2/1      1380 AM

The free play at this relatively new facility is literally that—gratis, year-round, for Okies and anyone else. "Everyone," says a regular, "wants to jump higher than the next one." Win by two, but watch out for the fifteen-minute limit that's sometimes in effect.

12TH AVENUE REC CENTER
12TH N.E. AND ROBINSON
NORMAN, OKLAHOMA

4/2   1400 AM

The word's out that there are no youth leagues here. Thus, there's lots of free-play time, and a mature type predominates.

MEMORIAL PARK
N.W. 36TH AND WESTERN
OKLAHOMA CITY, OKLAHOMA

 2/1      107.1 FM

Up from hackerdom! This spot, which earned the dreaded boot last go-round, now features the best evening runs in town. The tennis court lights filter over to the wood, so if you eat your carrots, you should dominate.

PARKS AND REC GYM
EAST 9TH AND LOWERY
STILLWATER, OKLAHOMA

4/2 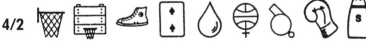 93.9 FM

Since nonstudents can't avail themselves of the facilities at Oklahoma State, this spot—open to all—gets good use.

MABEE CENTER PRACTICE GYM
ORAL ROBERTS UNIVERSITY
TULSA, OKLAHOMA

6/3  96.5 FM

The regular game here every Tuesday evening, year-round, is peopled with ministry employees who are devout backers of ''The Man.'' Says one player, ''We remain on our best behavior at all times. Except when we cuss, throw chairs, or punch out a radical opponent.''

TURNER REC CENTER
3503 EAST 5TH
TULSA, OKLAHOMA

4/1  96.5 FM

An earnest crowd shows on Tuesday and Thursday mornings, 9 to noon. They're serious about their call, in addition to their ball, so bring your lawyer. Or chuck it all and truck to Springdale Rec Center, where it's nothing but ball.

Tulsa *There's a heavy caseload at the Turner Rec Center court, where no one wants to take the rap and everyone dishes it out. (Rhonda Freiner)*

OREGON

DIXON REC CENTER
OREGON STATE UNIVERSITY
CORVALLIS, OREGON

6/3   106.1 FM

The place to play in town, though a fairly sterile spot with an equally predictable crowd. If you're not with the college, cross your fingers when trying to enter.

WASHINGTON-JEFFERSON STREET BRIDGE COURTS
JEFFERSON AND 1ST
EUGENE, OREGON

 6/3   96 FM

These courts are covered, so there's no need to worry about that ubiquitous rainfall. If you're having bad luck with hoop and ball, try the horseshoe pitch nearby, where "almost" counts.

BLUE MOUNTAIN GYM
BLUE MOUNTAIN COMMUNITY COLLEGE
PENDLETON, OREGON

8/4   90.9 FM

Games here can get wild and woolly. Once you're in the gym, there's free access to the indoor pool.

164

IRVING PARK
N.E. 7TH AND FREEMONT
PORTLAND, OREGON

 16/8   97.1 FM

Part of this complex, Portland's largest and most competitive, is covered and features lights. The whole place is usually full on weekend evenings.

MT. SCOTT COMMUNITY CENTER
5530 S.E. 72ND
PORTLAND, OREGON

6/3   107 FM

Some say the summer league here is the Northwest's best. Could be; there's hardly any granola-style ball in evidence.

Portland *Great (Mount) Scott! They sure know how to taper off after a few runs. (Gregg Childs)*

SPARKS CENTER
WILLAMETTE UNIVERSITY
SALEM, OREGON

4/2   105.1 FM

Attracts a wealthy, professional crowd. Needless to say, the law school supplies the most argumentative and competitive participants.

Altoona *The Hill provides the thrills at Mansion Park's high-level summer league. (J. D. Cavrich)*

PENNSYLVANIA

MANSION PARK
MANSION AND 35TH
ALTOONA, PENNSYLVANIA

Thanks to a local convenience store, which donated a lighting system several years back, a huge summer league has evolved. Drop the peculiar name of Galen Bickel to impress the locals; he went for an even 100 in one game. All-name match-up: Superior Water Treatment vs. Mr. Bips.

TAYLOR GYM
LEHIGH UNIVERSITY
BETHLEHEM, PENNSYLVANIA

Czar of the noontime games is a fiftyish regular named George. He's a research chemist at a local steel mill, but is known around the gym as ''The Commissioner.'' Show him appropriate respect.

FAIRVIEW PARK
FAIRVIEW
EASTON, PENNSYLVANIA

Playing here can be like taking something to the cleaners; the lights are coin-op, so bring quarters. There's a popular summer league at Eddyside Park that features out-to-pasture Eastern League types.

GLADWYNE PLAYGROUND
YOUNG'S FORD
GLADWYNE, PENNSYLVANIA

 2/1      105.9 FM

This exclusive suburb's showcase court has played host to a Hollywood film maker, a college prez, and the offspring of stars of the worlds of sports and rock 'n' roll. Talk about Mainlining.

MYLES PARK
GERMANTOWN AND JOSHUA
LAFAYETTE HILL, PENNSYLVANIA

 6/3      105.9 FM

A line drive from the adjacent softball field once banked off the backboard and through the hoop. That would be a three-pointer to everyone—except park regular Jim Drucker, the erstwhile CBA commissioner, promotional whiz, and innovator extraordinaire, who probably would have found a way to award four *points.*

COLOR MEN

They're the Chick Hearns of the asphalt: The Reverend is the legendary provider of patter at the Baker League in Philly. The fellow at Lexington's Dirt Bowl goes into his "I *vant* your *blood*" routine whenever someone on the Transylvania University team scores a hoop. And the man on the mike at the Great Boston Shootout heralds a stop in the action with an emphatic, "Time will be *out*."

Of course, you hardly need a P.A. system to throw your own two cents in. Consider the spectator at the Rucker in Harlem who, on seeing a participant collide with one of the basket supports, yelled out, "Don't mess with that pole, man! Pole's been out there all winter!"

BRANDON PARK
FAIRVIEW
LANCASTER, PENNSYLVANIA

 8/4   1490

Weekend mornings are big for pick-up here, though a higher level of comp can be found evenings, indoors, at Franklin & Marshall's Mayser Center.

168

ATHLETIC FIELD
LINCOLN
LATROBE, PENNSYLVANIA

      1570 AM

Low-key hoop in a pleasant setting. You're encouraged to take the ball to the hole, after local product Arnold Palmer.

BOYS CLUB
YOUTH WAY
MEDIA, PENNSYLVANIA

           104 FM

Players from Jersey and Delaware regularly trek over to check things out. With some two dozen teams, the summer league is a beaut.

NARBERTH REC BOARD COURTS
HAVERFORD AND WYNNEWOOD
NARBERTH, PENNSYLVANIA

        105.3 FM

The league here, which has operated nonstop since 1946, is where a Villanova assistant named George Raveling stashed such prize recruits as Artis Gilmore and Howard Porter. The league today is being revived as a suburban high school showcase, and the borough manager promises a top-to-bottom overhaul of the facilities soon.

CARVER CENTER
ARCH AND JACOBY
NORRISTOWN, PENNSYLVANIA

         105.3 FM

This Carver is without The White Shadow, or any white shadows, for that matter. High school talent abounds.

PHILLY

Harvey Holiday giving Sixers' scores on the box between cuts of musty soul. A training breakfast of Tastykakes washed down with Frank's orange soda. A Baker League clash between Fox Trap Disco and Bubble Tunnel Car Wash. There's a real *culture* to the cult of street ball in this town, which turns out more Complete Guards than any other burg. From storied Haddington Rec Center in Overbrook, to Sherwood Rec in West Philly, to the fill-the-lanes fellas across the river in Camden, the backcourt guys can handle it *and* stick it, push it up *and* pick apart zones. Sonny (Tempo, Brent, Tempo) Hill runs four leagues in addition to the Baker, whose oral historians speak reverently of the night Earl Monroe and Bill Bradley both broke fifty against each other in the cellar of the Bright Hope Baptist Church. Aaaaaah-*men*.

FORREST SCHOOLYARD
4300 ALDINE
PHILADELPHIA, PENNSYLVANIA

 4/2  **99 FM**

A real fossil: an urban run with an all-white crowd. A lot of pick-and-roll, give-and-go half court.

JARDEL REC CENTER
COTTMAN AND PENWAY
PHILADELPHIA, PENNSYLVANIA

 4/2 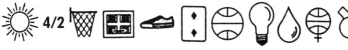 **105.3**

A facility for all seasons. Old-timers on Sundays, and class-cutting kids on weekdays; serious hoop all summer long, and kids wielding snow shovels during the winter. They clear away the white stuff to break in their new Christmas basketballs.

SHEPARD REC CENTER
HAVERFORD AND 57TH
PHILADELPHIA, PENNSYLVANIA

2/1  **105.3 FM**

This spot, the name of which was changed to honor a local minister, is still known as "Haddington" to those who watched Wilt Chamberlain and Sonny Hill come up here. The fervor has faded some, though an outdoor slab with eight racks and two full courts has been upgraded substantially.

SHERWOOD REC CENTER
CHRISTIAN AND 56TH
PHILADELPHIA, PENNSYLVANIA

6/3   105.3 FM

Philly's most phamous. And how's this for dunkproofing? The super intentionally sets the rims above ten feet, figuring routine jamming'll bring 'em into line.

DAVIS PARK
5670 HOBART
PITTSBURGH, PENNSYLVANIA

 2/1   105.9 FM

A lot of hacking, if not many hackers. Even the nets suffer; their life expectancy is never more than a week.

GARLAND PARK
EAST LIBERTY AND PENN
PITTSBURGH, PENNSYLVANIA

 3/1      105.9 FM

You can still find good runs at East Hills and Mellon parks (see IYF), but the garland's now worn by this spot, which has taken in the Connie Hawkins League. Police are dispatched to league games for crowd control—all things considered, a good sign.

OZANAM CULTURAL CENTER
WYLIE
PITTSBURGH, PENNSYLVANIA

 4/2    105.9 FM

Ozanam has seen some of the quickest, baddest, and best in the likes of Norm Nixon, Maurice Lucas, and Connie Hawkins. Serious ball, played

seriously, in Pittsburgh's notorious Hill District. The same crowd some-times airs it out at Reizenstein Schoolyard on East Liberty.

ROTARY COURT
20TH AND MAHANTONGO
POTTSVILLE, PENNSYLVANIA

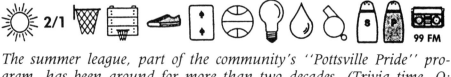

The summer league, part of the community's ''Pottsville Pride'' pro-gram, has been around for more than two decades. (Trivia time. Q: Name the former NFLer and former major-leaguer who have played here. A: Jack Dolbin, Denver Broncos; Lance Rautzhan, L.A. Dodgers.)

Pottsville *At Rotary Court players quote that upstand-ing Rotarian Kurtis Blow: ''You can't check me!''* (Harry Folino)

3RD AND SPRUCE REC CENTER
3RD AND SPRUCE
READING, PENNSYLVANIA

6/3

102.5 FM

Reading's main run. Between 1 and 3 every afternoon, shift workers fill the gym. The high schoolers and nine-to-fivers play at night.

GALVIN TERRACE
MULBERRY AND LINDEN
SCRANTON, PENNSYLVANIA

 4/2

590 AM

Pick-up games can be open-ended if no one's waiting. Someone, however, is usually down, so be prepared to call a halt to matters at 11. The summer league is first-rate.

Turtle Creek *Girls in the Top Cagers league are no stiffs, even if the Community Rec Center's so small that pregame stretching must take place on the grounds of a neighboring funeral home. (Times-Express/Gateway Publications)*

COMMUNITY REC CENTER
519 PENN
TURTLE CREEK, PENNSYLVANIA

6/3   96 FM

The gym is a shoe box, but players and spectators shoehorn themselves in for the Top Cagers girls' summer league. Among the fans: many senior citizens from the high rise across the street.

REC HALL
PENN STATE UNIVERSITY
UNIVERSITY PARK, PENNSYLVANIA

8/4    103 FM

The play can get pretty rough, especially if any of Paterno's players get into a game. The Parkhill brothers, homegrown hoopsters extraordinaire, own every angle and dead spot in the building when they choose to show. Bruce Parkhill, the Penn State coach, should have sympathy for those who sneak in; as a kid, he did, too.

FIELD HOUSE
VILLANOVA UNIVERSITY
VILLANOVA, PENNSYLVANIA

4/2   93.3 FM

The 'Cat House purrs with action during the summers, when Philly's finest—including a town of 'Nova resident named Julius—join the fray.

COLE STREET COMPLEX
COLE AND NORTH SHERMAN
WILKES-BARRE, PENNSYLVANIA

 4/2    98.5 FM

Summer runs are best, and they unfold 5 P.M. to 8 P.M. Similar comp can be found at Miner Park in South Wilkes-Barre.

RHODE ISLAND

TOWN COURTS
1ST
EAST GREENWICH, RHODE ISLAND

 4/2   92.3 FM

Hoops at "E.G.," as this spot is known, is all business. Post play gets fierce, and foul calls won't be met with sympathy. A Friday night tradition: a pick-up squad from Warwick, the adjoining town, challenges the E.G. regulars. Losers spring for the keg.

BASE GYM
NEWPORT NAVAL BASE
NEWPORT, RHODE ISLAND

 10/5      95.5 FM

All you need is a driver's license to get on base; once inside, you'll find plenty of action, including ratballer-for-life Kevin Stacom, whose establishment, The Dockside Saloon, is an obligatory postgame stop. If you're over thirty, white, and not Kevin Stacom, try the game at The Hut, on Spring Street.

SWENSON COURTS
SMITH
NORTH PROVIDENCE, RHODE ISLAND

 4/2      92.3 FM

Just resurfaced, with new vapor lighting installed. Says Charles, who's right-hand man to Lou, the summer-league commish here at Evans

Field: "We're nationally ranked." Attracts any former Providence College hoopster worth his salt.

JOHN STREET PLAYGROUND
JOHN AND INDUSTRIAL
PAWTUCKET, RHODE ISLAND

 4/2   92.3 FM

The most popular hours are 5 to 8 on summer evenings, though those wanting top comp may have already bolted for Providence by then. Expect contact inside on anything.

PETERSON REC CENTER
PROVIDENCE COLLEGE
PROVIDENCE, RHODE ISLAND

10/5   92.3 FM

If you can't find a run to your liking in this new complex, check out the eight hoops in the old one. It'll cost you $250 a year if you're not PC-affiliated.

CASS PARK
CASS
WOONSOCKET, RHODE ISLAND

 2/1   1240 AM

Games are run straight if anyone's waiting with winners. A blacker game is played at Dunn Park; another good run can be found at Cold Spring Park.

For these cagers at Chicago's Metropolitan Correctional Center, playing yardbird is a rare chance to fly. (Geoffrey Biddle/Archive)

SLAMMER JAMMERS

This isn't a game you'll necessarily want to get into. Then again, while the food's worse than what you'll find on the outside, and the social life is worse, and such minor things as life expectancy are worse, too, the ball—dare we say it?—just may be better.

Prison-yard culture spawns nicknames, just like schoolyard society. Ask the Trotters about the bundle of buckets they surrendered at Attica to Kind John, so named because he *didn't* off the fellow inmate he'd caught pilfering his cigarettes. Moses Malone banged with the prison crowd in Petersburg, Virginia, particularly with The Milkman, so called " 'cause he murdered a milkman, man.''

The last word belongs to an inmate at the Metropolitan Correctional Center, a sky-rise federal clink in downtown Chitown, where prisoners while away as much of their sentences as possible at the outdoor slab on the twenty-sixth floor.

"You realize you've got the highest court in Chicago?''

"We were *put* here by the highest court in Chicago, too.''

SOUTH CAROLINA

BOYKIN PARK
CAMPBELL
CAMDEN, SOUTH CAROLINA

A royal spot, laid out by King Charles more than 200 years ago. But the real landmarks are nearby Belton's Grocery, and the incomparable Tessie's Restaurant, renowned for its home cooking.

CITY GYM
81 HAGOOD
CHARLESTON, SOUTH CAROLINA

The regulars give something back here: they're assessed $5 a year, two bucks of which goes toward one youth membership. The ladies step out on Sunday nights, and league play rages throughout the winter.

MITCHELL PARK
ROUTE 17 AND RUTLEDGE
CHARLESTON, SOUTH CAROLINA

With the park sitting right off the highway, the exit ramp provides handy access for travelers. As is the pattern in Dixie, best runs take place at twilight.

FIKE FIELDHOUSE
CLEMSON UNIVERSITY
CLEMSON, SOUTH CAROLINA

 6/3   1560 AM

No truth to the rumor that this is called the Probate Court. During the summer, with guys like Larry Nance and Chubby Wells playing, its reputation is beyond reproach.

SOLOMON BLATT P.E. CENTER
UNIVERSITY OF SOUTH CAROLINA
COLUMBIA, SOUTH CAROLINA

 4/2      104.7 FM

The pick-up never drops off. Gamecocks picking up academic slack during the summer still get their hoop in during the evenings, while three courts outdoors accommodate the less rarefied, including frat and townie types.

COMMUNITY CENTER
OLD MONCK'S CORNER
GOOSE CREEK, SOUTH CAROLINA

 6/3    95 FM

Goose Creek ripples with play the year round. The super, LeBon, will point out a game to suit your strengths.

ARMORY GYM
401 EAST PARK
GREENVILLE, SOUTH CAROLINA

 6/3   1070 AM

Shoot your bank shots with due respect; they're striking the very boards off which Frank Selvy scored 100 points while at Furman. You can look it up.

179

Hilton Head Island *At the Youth Center Court, the crib is full because the house rule is straight up.*

COURTHOUSE ANNEX
WILLIAM HILTON
HILTON HEAD ISLAND, SOUTH CAROLINA

 2/1    93.1 FM

The homeboys include a nasty brood of shakers and bakers. Be sure one of the better debaters is on your side, because there's plenty of on-court litigation. If someone says the score is "four-tray," don't panic; that's just "four-three" in Gullah, the local dialect.

YOUTH CENTER COURT
CORDILLO AND DEALLYON
HILTON HEAD ISLAND, SOUTH CAROLINA

 1/0    93.1 FM

Springtime, vacationing college students pick pick-up play up. Parking-lot security lights let late-shift food-and-beverage types get in a little pre- and postwork action. Keep your reflexes sharp, for bounds and steals go straight up.

ST. ANDREW'S CATHOLIC SCHOOL PARKING LOT
36TH
MYRTLE BEACH, SOUTH CAROLINA

         3/1 101.7 FM

A high-school hangout, with a lot of suburbanized bros and CYO types. As at most Catholic-school parking lots, hooping is prohibited from 4 P.M. Saturday (5 o'clock mass) 'til 3 P.M. Sunday.

DUPONT OUTDOOR REC AREA
JACKSON AND WEST
NORTH AUGUSTA, SOUTH CAROLINA

2/1    104.3 FM

With a leaky roof, all runs are subject to rain delays. Games to 10, unless more than five would-be players are present, in which case games end at 7. This spot is a.k.a the Sno-Cap Coliseum, after the Sno-Cap Drive-In right across the street.

DUKES GYM
SOUTH CAROLINA STATE COLLEGE
ORANGEBURG, SOUTH CAROLINA

2/1    101.3 FM

Some of the best runs here are between local favorites and ex–college players. Is this a funky school or what? The intramural program includes a slam-dunk contest for players under 6'. Not something they do at BYU.

CLEVELAND PARK
CLEVELAND PARK AND ASHEVILLE
SPARTANBURG, SOUTH CAROLINA

 16/8    1530 AM

To ''take the train'' here may be something other than a violation, for a little passenger model chugs along a track around the park. Action can also be found at Irwin Park, and in the driveway of USC-Spartanburg coach Jerry Waters's home at 324 Shady Lane.

181

SOUTH DAKOTA

YMCA
LINCOLN
ABERDEEN, SOUTH DAKOTA

6/3

This Y is located downtown in a county called Brown, so take your Js from long range in honor of former SuperSonics guard Freddie.

JEFFERSON SCHOOLYARD
CENTRAL AND 5TH
PIERRE, SOUTH DAKOTA

 4/2

There's no drinking fountain, so you'll have to trudge by the softball field to wet your whistle. The City Auditorium is center stage for all indoor action.

STEVENS HIGH SCHOOL GYM
44TH AND RANGE
RAPID CITY, SOUTH DAKOTA

6/2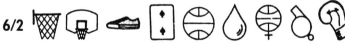

Reservations aren't required, though most who run here live on one. Nearby Ellsworth AFB has a gym that attracts a lofty clientele.

GYM
MOUNT MARTY COLLEGE
YANKTON, SOUTH DAKOTA

6/3  104.1 FM

The floor is tile and the walls abut the court's boundaries. Hold the complaints, however. It's slim pickings for a hoop junkie in this town.

DOERS' PROFILES (CONT.)

We looked at a dozen of them in *The In-Your-Face Basketball Book*—guys whose ability to do it made them worthy of profile, but whose dreams had for some reason gotten scotched. These doers weren't blacklisted, much less Black Labeled; they just never got their big break, even though all their homeboys knew they could play. We've kept up with two of them.

One is Boston's Steven Strother. He has left the Hub, but still gets precious little pub. Word reaches us that Stro is now playing his ball in L.A. where, he says, "I still fascinate myself."

The other is Lewis Lloyd. When we last checked up on Black Magic, he was stalking the back streets of Philly, weighing a chance to attend a military school in New Mexico, doing his damnedest to get it together. And didn't he, though? Made the NBA, after going to Drake, where he nearly led the nation in scoring twice. He even had a chance to visit the White House, where he met Jimmy Carter. The prez, the story goes, went from Drake player to Drake player, shaking hands and making introductions. "Pop Wright, sir," said one, as Carter moved on. "Tony Watson, sir," said another, and down the line the President went. Until he reached Lewis. "Lewis Lloyd, sir. The Magic Man, sir."

And it counts.

TENNESSEE

SLATER GYM
MCDOWELL
BRISTOL, TENNESSEE

2/1    1490 AM

An old gym with a creaky floor and wooden backboards. Appropriately enough, a few senior citizens have been known to stop by and shoot a few.

GLENWOOD REC CENTER
EAST 3RD AND GLENWOOD
CHATTANOOGA, TENNESSEE

6/3   1100 AM

The city's best players congregate here, though excellent runs take place at Washington Hills Rec Center and Tennessee-Chattanooga's MacLellan Gym.

RIVERVIEW COMMUNITY CENTER
LOUIS AND WHEATLEY
KINGSPORT, TENNESSEE

2/1    101.5 FM

They'll run from noon 'til lights out (that's 10 P.M.) outdoors in the summer, though another court in the adjacent gym awaits those who want refuge from the humidity.

Doc Overholt oversees operations at his backyard court in suburban Knoxville.

WHAT'S UP? DOC'S

Sometimes Dr. Robert Overholt will awake at 2 in the morning—or 3, even—and realize there's a full-bore run going on in his backyard. Occasionally he gets phone calls from people who'll say, "You don't know me, but I just wanna say 'thank you.'" And sometimes he'll be up at 5, set to go to the Knoxville office where he works as an allergist, only to find a couple of people shooting a few out back. He assumes they've been there all night.

Doc Overholt doesn't mind. He *can't* mind, really, for he's the one who installed that lighted mecca in 1976 and issued a standing invitation to the world. "Dr. Overholt's," as it's known, sits down the slope of a five-acre plot behind a stately home in Knoxville's fashionable West Hills section. Doc, as *he's* known, pays the monthly lighting bills, changes the nets, and plots ways to bring a water line closer to courtside to cure parched throats. It's all a hobby, a diversion from curing wheezin' and sneezin'.

Several summers back Overholt went so far as to promote a tournament, billed as Doc's Shootout, to which just about everyone, including most local college players, was invited. The NCAA put the kibosh on that, but Doc's has nonetheless become the place to run in east Tennessee. Among those who've played are Bernard King, Ernie Grunfeld, Dale Ellis, and a fair number of Tennessee Vols past and present, and even such regional studfish as Baskerville Holmes and Cedric Henderson. Talk about making housecalls.

During hooping weather, Sunday night brings out the best comp, with Mondays a close second. Then matters taper off as the week wears on, only to get geared up again the following Sunday. The rules are few and simple: call your own; spirit, but no spirits; and, please, no profanity. The only oaths the Good Doctor will suffer are Hippocratic ones.

DR. OVERHOLT'S
BROOME AND KEMPTON
KNOXVILLE, TENNESSEE

 2/1

See-through boards, ample parking, and the authentic atmosphere of affluence, any time you want. Ernie Grunfeld has called the Good Doctor's "the best outdoor court I've ever seen."

HPER BUILDING
UNIVERSITY OF TENNESSEE
KNOXVILLE, TENNESSEE

10/5

The sign says NO DUNKING ALLOWED WHILE PLAYING BASKETBALL, *which we assume means it's O.K. to jam while playing P-Funk or the Bar-Kays. IDs start getting checked around 3 in the afternoon, so if you're not legit, get there early.*

LINDEN PARK
LINDEN AND CRUZE
KNOXVILLE, TENNESSEE

 4/2

Some of the better players who once hung out here now avoid it because the physical play has gotten out of hand. Half court predominates, played according to "Kentucky rules," as straight-up is known in these parts.

BLUFF-CITY BALL

Some consider it second-fiddle to country cousin Nashville in musical matters, but Memphis hardly deserves a bad rap in hoops, where there's no singing the blues. The schoolyards aren't yards *per se,* just poured concrete out back, but they're crawling just the same. And there's a citywide system of user-friendly parks and gym-equipped community centers, where half the citizenry seems to get after it. "This is the nest-bed," says one Memphian. "It's *hot.*" Sho'nuff is Saturday mornings, when the old-timers rock each other at O'Brien Park and a down is an elusive, precious thing; and when Coach Dorsey's sports report on the Southern Giant, 1030 AM, all but tells you where they be running at.

BRENTWOOD PARK
SPOTSWOOD AND PENDLETON
MEMPHIS, TENNESSEE

The spot to rock around the clock in the Orange Mound section of town. The games go as long as the lights go, which is to say 'til 3 A.M.

WESTWOOD COMMUNITY CENTER
810 WESTERN PARK
MEMPHIS, TENNESSEE

With twenty-five community centers to choose from, we're hard-pressed to single out one run. But Westwood attracts more than its share of wizardry, and Gaston Community Center is a worthy backup.

ALUMNI MEMORIAL GYM
MIDDLE TENNESSEE STATE
MURFREESBORO, TENNESSEE

College gyms usually go by ''Alumni'' or ''Memorial,'' not both, but we can understand it if they're a bit confused here. So much throwing down goes down that racks have to be put back in line once a month.

GENTRY CENTER
TENNESSEE STATE UNIVERSITY
NASHVILLE, TENNESSEE

Home to the Stephens Summer League, central Tennessee's finest. Truck (Robinson) on down and Phil (Hubbard) it up. Ample AC and seating make it a dog-days delight. High schoolers run out of the gym at Aquinas J.C.

Oak Ridge *With a couple of fence-hangers always ready to mix it up, comp at Scarboro's more than fair.*

SCARBORO COMMUNITY CENTER
CARVER AND WILBERFORCE
OAK RIDGE, TENNESSEE

 4/2   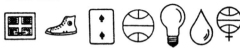   1290 AM

The elder folk play on the court with the square backboards. Among players of all ages, games are almost always half court.

TEXAS

SEARS REC CENTER
2400 AMBLER
ABILENE, TEXAS

2/1   107.9 FM

An exceptionally clean facility, where everything, showers included, is free. You may catch Harvey Catchings, too.

BONESHOOKS PARK
N.W. 20TH AND HUGHES
AMARILLO, TEXAS

 4/2   93.1 FM

Boneshooks was a storied black cowboy and breaker of wild horses who was raised in the Panhandle. Without nets, the hoops look like lonely lariats, but some bucking goes on by those trying to put balls through them.

MEADOWBROOK GYM
1300 DUGAN
ARLINGTON, TEXAS

2/1   104 FM

A wide range of talent, from the All-America to the All-Neighborhood. Bros pay respect to whites who bang.

189

Austin *At the University of Texas's Clark Field, the pick-up roundup takes place late every afternoon. J 'em Horns.*

CLARK FIELD
UNIVERSITY OF TEXAS
AUSTIN, TEXAS

 8/4   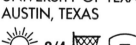      98.3 FM

The gates to this spot, which has one hoop at fantasy height, are open 10 to 10 weekends, noon to 10 weekdays. Alas, they're beginning to check for IDs. Abe Lemons would be appalled if he knew . . .

WEST ENFIELD PARK
ENFIELD AND WINSTED
AUSTIN, TEXAS

 2/1      98.3 FM

With the court hard by a freeway off ramp, openings in "up" games here get filled quickly. The slippery concrete surface is good for sliding D, bad for gliding O.

190

LINCOLN CENTER
1000 ELEANOR
COLLEGE STATION, TEXAS

8/4   94.3 FM

Boast to the Janis Ians of the world that you've played Lincoln Center, an old black high school that has been remodeled. The floor gets slick in humid weather, so be careful; there are no towel boys.

T. C. AYERS REC CENTER
1722 WINNEBAGO
CORPUS CHRISTI, TEXAS

 4/2   105 FM

Even if these courts are right behind the police station, you should be forewarned of the neighborhood's toughness. The pro footballers who play here, like Riley Odoms and Robert Newhouse, don't have to worry.

FRETZ PARK REC CENTER
BELTLINE AND HILLCREST
DALLAS, TEXAS

6/3   98 FM

A solid run in an air-conditioned gym. Very little arguing goes on among this clubby, racially balanced crowd. If this place is locked up, check out Reverchon Rec Center, which never is.

MARTIN LUTHER KING COMMUNITY CENTER
OAKLAND AND PEABODY
DALLAS, TEXAS

8/4   104 FM

Management would appreciate it if, once you get up, you'd kindly heed the NO DUNKING *warnings stenciled to the backboards, and just lay the rock in. A more hospitable sign welcomes you to "The Kingdome," which is so heavily used that an outdoor court is in the planning stages. Also cruise Redbird Rec Center, where the Metroplex's Pro-Am is headquartered.*

CENTER GYM
FORT BLISS
EL PASO, TEXAS

6/3   **920 AM**

The mix is black, white, and Mexican, with a dollop of seasoning from the UTEP varsity. Comp is particularly Blissful on weekends.

WRIGHT-CUMY PARK
718 41ST
GALVESTON, TEXAS

 8/4    **1400 AM**

Rainy days shouldn't keep you away, nor should outrageously hot ones. It's an all-weather roof.

HOUSTON

Before Angelo at Fondé, there was Bruzz at Finnegan. Bruzz Henry ruled the city's fifth ward until his death in the early '70s, directing and teaching and encouraging kids from his roost at Finnegan Rec Center. Things changed one year after a bunch of U of H players were turned out of the old Jeppesen Field House on campus because the floor was being resurfaced; they scooted over to Fondé and one local institution replaced the other. There's a surprising amount of team ball at Fondé, and it carries over to other runs in the city. Players make that extra pass because they feel the need to ingratiate themselves, to establish a cadre of "running mates" who'll be sure to choose one another should one of them have a precious "up" game. In other words, they hope the favor, if not necessarily the pass, will be returned.

FINNEGAN PARK
SONORA AND PROVIDENCE
HOUSTON, TEXAS

 6/3    **102 FM**

This place was once as mythical as Fondé, back when the pros hung here off-season, and Wheatley High (it's across the street) had the finest five in the land. Things have fallen off some, though there are still good runs to be had on Wednesdays and Saturdays. There's also a full court available indoors.

FONDE REC CENTER
SABINE AND MEMORIAL
HOUSTON, TEXAS

6/3 102 FM

Monday, Monday—you can trust that day here, because that's when the seriosi show. Angelo decides who gets to run, so butter up the man as best you can.

Fondé's heap big chief is Angelo Cascio, the man who decides who ranks where on the Houston totem pole.

FONDE'S FOUNDING FATHER

Before making your way into the gym at Fondé Rec Center, take a look around. See if you can't tell why this place, which sits just beyond the shadows cast by downtown Houston's skyscrapers, is special. There's the parking lot, which on a summer's night will be filled with second-hand Chevys and shimmering Mercedeses and Rollses—not a single middle-class machine. There's the quote on the facade that reads: "Recreation, like religion, should permeate all of life." But nothing sums up Fondé's essence as felicitously as the stand of totem poles out front. It has been called The Best Little Basketball Gym in Texas, and thanks to a 5'5" septuagenarian named Angelo Cascio, it's also the most hierarchical pick-up spot in the nation.

With his white hair and black horn-rims, Cascio would suggest a frumpy Cary Grant were it not for his having had the same wife for half a century. Yet for half of that half-century, Fondé has been Angelo's mistress, luring him from his job at an envelope company to supervise the gym on weekday evenings.

He doles out no more than a handful of "ups" each night, usually to the owners of the elegant rides out front, which is to say to Moses and

Akeem and Clyde the Glide. They, in turn, can pick anyone they want to run with them. Only if the pros don't show to claim the games will the names of the more mortal regulars—they sport good Texas nicknames like Horsehead and Cochise—go down on the Cascio clipboard. "If it's your 'up,'" says Lott Brooks, a local lawyer and one of the Fondé faithful, "you *want* Moses to walk in the door."

Angelo's quality control keeps the pros around, the chumps (he calls 'em "rinky-dinks") out, and anyone from getting hurt, but also occasionally forces some very good ballplayers to sit through an entire evening. Someone once griped to City Hall about Angelo's elitism, and there was a movement afoot to replace him with a more equal-opportunity-minded super. But the bureaucrats eventually realized that they couldn't mess with an institution, particularly one who commands so much respect. There's no booze, no drugs, little profanity, and no fights. "They fight," Angelo says, "they know I take 'em to the *police* station right across the street."

MACGREGOR PARK
CALHOUN AND MACGREGOR SOUTH
HOUSTON, TEXAS

The lights—and the games—luminesce 'til 2 A.M. under the Taco Bell–style pavilion roof here, just steps away from where in-your-face tennis queen Zina Garrison learned her game. As they say, different strokes . . .

Houston *Like Tex-Mex food, the days at MacGregor Park can get awfully hot, so the Spanish mission architecture is appreciated.*

SUNSET PARK
SUNSET AND BELMONT
HOUSTON, TEXAS

 2/1   102 FM

The official name for this spot, in Rick Barry's old neighborhood, is Wein Park, but no one calls it that. A short court, with best runs early Friday evenings. At Fleming Park, down Sunset at Kent, two half courts serve a lot of Rice students and faculty.

SENTER PARK REC CENTER
900 SOUTH CENTER
IRVING, TEXAS

8/4   106 FM

The oldest and largest gym in Irving is in the southeast part of town. Lots of free-play time, with half court preferred. In fact, pick-up is so popular, there's no need for leagues. (At the other extreme is Austin Rec Center, a "better-call-first" facility, which operates at irregular hours and limits pick-up times because of heavy league-play bookings. Austin's women's summer league is one of the country's best.)

P.E. BUILDING
UNIVERSITY OF TEXAS
SAN ANTONIO, TEXAS

4/2    1480 AM

You'd think The Iceman (a regular) would be the most storied product of this spot, which is numero uno in San Antone. In fact, it's James, a.k.a. The Whistler (you can always hear him coming), who has funky duds but mismatched moves.

BLEDSOE-MILLER REC CENTER
300 BRAZOS
WACO, TEXAS

2/1      95.5 FM

A Texas-size bunch of Texas-size gridders, including Mike Singletary, won't let you forget where hoop ranks in this state.

UTAH

DECAFFEINATED HOOP

Say this for Mormons: you've got to play by their rules, but they love their hoop and they're hospitable folk. Anyone can get a game almost anywhere at "The Y," which in these parts refers not to the YMCA, but to Brigham Young University. And "ward ball," a sort of Latter-Day-Saints CYO, is fiercely played all over Utah, too.

If you're not part of the BYU community, you'll have to plunk down the requisite couple of bucks to rent a standard-issue BYU gym uniform. (You've also got to wear it; if you don't, floating bouncers will thumb you out, unless you happen to be one of the oversized Samoans of the sort who flout the rule a lot, and with whom few floating bouncers mess.) You'll also be introduced to "Winners After Six," which isn't a new tuxedo line, but an idiosyncrasy of make it, take it. You play half court by ones to thirty, losers out, and win by two—but whoever reaches six baskets first gets make it, take it privileges for the rest of the game.

Just about every LDS church has a multipurpose rec hall, most of which are, by church edict, carpeted, so as to better accommodate ladies' quilting sessions and the like. Dribbling on carpet is tricky and, as one regular attests, "you can get some serious burns." Mormons are legendary for their industriousness, so you'll find some of the best games as early as 6 A.M.

MARSHALL WHITE COMMUNITY CENTER
28TH AND LINCOLN
OGDEN, UTAH

6/3  1430 AM

The sole indoor community center in town attracts a good run. A surprisingly large Hispanic clientele for Mormon country.

Provo *Mormon modesty doesn't prohibit shirts 'n' skins, but that's about the only informality you'll find in a faculty run at BYU's Smith Fieldhouse.*

SMITH FIELDHOUSE (EAST GYM)
BRIGHAM YOUNG UNIVERSITY
PROVO, UTAH

12/6    96.1 FM

From noon to 1 and 3:30 to 5, BYU faculty and staff have dibs. Also, check out the old varsity court in the same building. The Globetrotters, who are the Mormons' equal in getting around to people, loved its spring so much they called it the best court they'd ever played on.

DESERET GYM
161 NORTH MAIN
SALT LAKE CITY, UTAH

12/6    98.7 FM

ALL YOU CAN BEAT FOR $3.25. *That's what you'll pay per day to run at the "D.G." The rules have more teeth than the Osmond family.*

SPORTS MALL METRO
SOUTH TEMPLE AND MAIN
SALT LAKE CITY, UTAH

4/2    1320 AM

To paraphrase Brigham Young himself, "This is the place," in a major downtown shopping mall. Three-on-three full-court is popular—and possible, because courts are short. Problem is, everyone's ready to call a foul, but no one's willing to call out a screen.

VERMONT

SOUTH PARK
LOCUST
BURLINGTON, VERMONT

 4/2      1390 AM

Newly renovated, with a steady stream of summertime play. When the temp turns chilly—that's from August to May—the same crowd migrates to the Y. Over there, things never really get hot, but, being Vermont, there's a thaw of sorts in March, when a big tournament takes place. Check out the jogging track overhead, where local Socialist politico Bernie Sanders has been seen. He can't go to his right.

DANA THOMPSON MEMORIAL PARK
ROUTE 30
MANCHESTER CENTER, VERMONT

 4/2      97.1 FM

Cruise the highway toward Dorset, and you can't miss it. Mountains, sky, trees, and lots of schoolboys from Burr & Burton, the Green Mountain State's high school power. Post hoop, spring for the two bucks to use the adjacent pool.

BARLOW STREET PLAYGROUND
BARLOW AND WELDEN
ST. ALBANS, VERMONT

 2/1      95 FM

With racks that politely bow to 9'6'', many a Green Mountain Boy can get syrupy over the possibilities.

198

GEORGE RATCLIFFE PARK
NUTT AND ELM
WHITE RIVER JUNCTION, VERMONT

 2/1   1400 AM

Hackers' delight. Watch out for Dean, who uses his arms as buzz saws and would just as soon dispatch any pantywaist who dares call a foul to Petticoat *Junction.*

WOODSTOCK REC CENTER
54 RIVER
WOODSTOCK, VERMONT

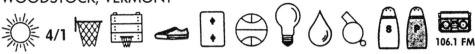 4/1   106.1 FM

The authors' home court, where In-Your-Face *began. Like good Moslems, we face The Stock several times a day, bow our heads, and say our incantations. All zealotry aside, the court is certifiably gorgeous, and the league is still known throughout these parts as "East Central Vermont's Premier Summer Event."*

Woodstock *Yankee reserve often goes by the boards in The Stock, where a summer league megatilt can deliver a throng to the Rec Center court.*

VIRGINIA

CHARLES HOUSTON REC CENTER
ROUTE 1 AND WYTHE
ALEXANDRIA, VIRGINIA

 6/3      **96.3 FM**

The solid metro-D.C. comp includes the redoubtable Little Willie, a terrific point guard who treats the wood here as if it were his studio. Wednesday's ''Ladies Night,'' while the over-thirty crowd tends to confine itself to the less-intense runs at the Patrick Henry Center. The motto there: Give me hoops or give me death.

WAR MEMORIAL GYM
VIRGINIA TECH
BLACKSBURG, VIRGINIA

 12/6      **104.9 FM**

Why do the best players always run on the court closest to the doors? 'Cause they fling the portals open in the summertime, the better to cool out. Best runs midafternoon, year-round.

THE DELL
UNIVERSITY OF VIRGINIA
CHARLOTTESVILLE, VIRGINIA

 6/3      **97.5 FM**

A notch below Slaughter, UVa's favored indoor run, this spot is populated by frat types, local high schoolers, and streetballers. Beware: (1) the pole, which has claimed many a victim; and (2) Sherm the Worm, a retired quarterback and active enforcer.

Harrisonburg *The only homeboy who needn't watch out for a bounder's stray bow at the Community Activities Center is a 7'4" guy named Ralph. (Patricia Huffman)*

MARTIN-BROCK GYM
EMORY AND HENRY COLLEGE
EMORY, VIRGINIA

2/1   **101 FM**

The entire campus is a historical landmark, and the gym an architectural curiosity. Fortunately, serious townies dilute the E&H preppies on the court. We can't imagine why you'd want to gawk, but the track that circles above the court provides a good vantage point.

COMMUNITY ACTIVITIES CENTER
305 SOUTH DOGWOOD
HARRISONBURG, VIRGINIA

6/3   **1360 AM**

The place to play in town. Homeboy Ralph Sampson dipped his tiny head under the gym doorway more than once.

PEAKSVIEW PARK
ARDMORE
LYNCHBURG, VIRGINIA

2/1   **101.7 FM**

A fetching, relatively modern court within a huge park. Runs go to twenty, even when there are sometimes as many as fifty people awaiting a game.

DORRIE MILLER GYM
WICKHAM
NEWPORT NEWS, VIRGINIA

2/1      102.9 FM

Come ready to play, because the line forms to the rear, and it's a line. Attracts the best from Hampton as well as Newport News.

THE ARENA
GRANBY AND VIRGINIA BEACH
NORFOLK, VIRGINIA

2/1      102.9 FM

They call it "the midday retreat," the noontime run occasionally patronized by the guy who had a cup of coffee in the pros. Everything goes to seven, so "nexts" isn't something you'll sit with for long. If your collar's white, stick to the Bute Street Y.

MARINE BARRACKS GYM
NORFOLK NAVAL BASE
NORFOLK, VIRGINIA

2/1      93.7 FM

Looking for a few good runs? The Marines go first class; the floor is NBA-quality, and the regulars maneuver at a high level. Games, needless to say, are rough. Over at the Naval Air Station Gym, you'll find lousy lighting and a warped, creaky floor.

LEE PARK
JOHNSON AND PARK
PETERSBURG, VIRGINIA

 4/2      99.3 F

An excellent run, with comp ranging from Moses Malone himself and a variety of Virginia's collegians, to local studfish. Games sometimes go 'til 3 A.M.

FRANKLIN STREET GYM
VIRGINIA COMMONWEALTH UNIVERSITY
RICHMOND, VIRGINIA

6/3      1540 AM

Hoops in this city are on a major uptick, and many of Virginia's finest take care of business during the off-season at this spot. Sunday mornings, however, the scene shifts to the gym at John Marshall High, where Fred Bibby, Henry's brother, has the key.

COMMON SCENTS

Ballplayers, especially those of the street variety, are an energetic breed not always content to confine their shakes and bakes to the macadam. Squeeze a little hoop in before work; squeeze a little *more* in before, well, before cavorting with the tender gender. No time for hygienic niceties like showers. So more and more guys are cruising the discount stores and drugettes, scoring one of those little thimble-size capsules of dab-on cologne (they're usually up front, near the register) before going off to take care of business. You're hooped out, but no one's grossed out. Just a li'l dab'll do ya.

PINE CAMP REC PARK
OLD BROOK
RICHMOND, VIRGINIA

 4/2      1540 AM

Draws an interneighborhood crowd. Because of this, forensic skills of two sorts are helpful; bring a rule book—and some formaldehyde. Says one local old-timer: "This isn't a Yankee ghetto. Whites are welcome, but they'd better be able to play." South Side, try Westover Playground; West End Playground has atmosphere to match the comp.

WAUSENA PARK
WILEY
ROANOKE, VIRGINIA

 4/1    910 AM

Virginia Tech players hardly consider it hokey to make the thirty-mile trek down here from campus. This is where the cream of the Commonwealth's small-college crop runs, and white guys should make sure they

can play. *Chill out at the 7-Eleven with local legend Man-Mountain Mike, and check out the By Invitation Only summer league at Jefferson High.*

VIRGINIA BEACH REC CENTER
MONMOUTH AND LOCKE
VIRGINIA BEACH, VIRGINIA

6/3  98.7 FM

Tightly supervised pick-up play—a Center staffer controls the ''down'' list—rages from noon to 3 weekdays. But the best tradition at this spot (which is technically in Kempsville) is the Monday and Wednesday night round-robin pick-up tournament, featuring the first thirty players through the door. That door opens at 6, so don't dawdle.

WASHINGTON

BCC GYM
BELLEVUE COMMUNITY COLLEGE
BELLEVUE, WASHINGTON

8/4    **93 FM**

The league here is O.K., even if it has about as much atmosphere as your local McDonald's. Just the same, it's reassuring to know that the NO DUNKING *signs are ignored.*

REC CENTER
CONTRA COSTA AND ELECTRON
FIRCREST, WASHINGTON

 2/1   **97.3 FM**

A very suburban spot, with the lushness of the Pacific Northwest evident all around. An indoor slab should help you cope with the elements.

OLD WASHINGTON GYM
LEGION AND EASTSIDE
OLYMPIA, WASHINGTON

6/3   **1240 AM**

A classic, homey court, where Norman (Paint) Rockwell would have run. It gets cold and drafty in the winter, but sun seeps through the large windows. ''We get brain surgeons side by side with loggers,'' says the super. A solid autumnal Sunday bunch of regulars runs 'til 1:30, when they adjourn to catch the Seahawks.

PASCO HIGH SCHOOL ACTIVITIES CENTER
HENRY AND 14TH
PASCO, WASHINGTON

8/4   94.9 FM

When the women come to play—and they do *come to* play*—all profanity stops. A dollar gets you in. Not many bros, but plenty of Mexican-Americans and American Indians.*

LIBERTY PARK
HOUSER AND BRONSON
RENTON, WASHINGTON

 3/1   89.5 FM

Fifteen hours of play a day during the summer, with this court's proximity to I-405 luring hoopsters off the highway. Pool and concession stand nearby.

I-5 FREEWAY COURTS
42ND AND INTERSTATE 5
SEATTLE, WASHINGTON

 2/1   93 FM

Sheltered from Seattle's frequently ugly elements, this under-the-freeway court has lights that put out as long as you do. You'll find a few players hanging on the rim, and a few just hanging out, like Detlef Schrempf, the titanic Teuton.

THE IMA
UNIVERSITY OF WASHINGTON
SEATTLE, WASHINGTON

8/4   89.5 FM

This building is the U. of W. (a.k.a "U-Dub") intramural facility. The best players gravitate to the north court, where it helps to know a little German (you may be playing with one). It also helps to know someone to vouch for you at the front desk.

Seattle *The rule at Montlake is no dunking, and the rim seems to be player enforcer it on a would-be Criminal Courts outlaw. But, hey, this isn't crime, just civil disobedience. (Susan Bassow)*

MONTLAKE REC CENTER
WEST MONTLAKE
SEATTLE, WASHINGTON

6/3    **89.5 FM**

We're not going to speculate as to why this spot is called the Criminal Courts. The play here is strictly "above board." Which is to say that on occasion the players get up pretty high.

UNDER-THE-FREEWAY COURTS
4TH AND MCCLELLAN
SPOKANE, WASHINGTON

 6/3    **92.9 FM**

Noisy and dirty, but the most popular place to play in eastern Washington. Best of all, no rainouts.

207

SPRINKER REC CENTER
SOUTH C AND MILITARY
TACOMA, WASHINGTON

 8/4   97.3 FM

Showers of the non-meteorological variety are available after games, which run to twenty by twos. A lovely park setting that's great for spectating.

DAVID DOUGLAS PARK
NORTH GARRISON
VANCOUVER, WASHINGTON

 4/2    93.3 FM

The courts are relatively new, but occasional bouts with vandals may put a backboard out of commission.

MILLER PARK
NORTH 4TH
YAKIMA, WASHINGTON

 2/1      107.3 FM

The main slab hereabouts, with a swimming pool nearby. Great chain nets make every swish sound like a dude out of Dickens is sixth man.

WEST VIRGINIA

INTERSTATE COURTS
DONNALLY AT I-77/79/64 INTERSECTION
CHARLESTON, WEST VIRGINIA

 4/2  950 AM

It's all here: rest rooms, bleachers, a concession stand, and a summer league. You can play rain or shine, as the courts sit under a freeway. Now, in a monsoon, you might consider going indoors, to the Central Charleston Community Center, which is right next door.

WINDMILL PARK
MAPLE
FAIRMONT, WEST VIRGINIA

 4/2  106 FM

You won't find local-girl-made-good Mary Lou Retton doing floor exercises on the sidelines, but you may find the occasional breakdancer. Lots of players cruise this spot to show off their rides.

SCOTT COMMUNITY CENTER
8TH
HUNTINGTON, WEST VIRGINIA

 2/1  100.5 FM

In the center of The Block, as Huntington's black neighborhood is known. See if you can hang with the evening regulars—and hang with the gang that hews to Meminger's Law.

209

STANSBERRY HALL
UNIVERSITY OF WEST VIRGINIA
MORGANTOWN, WEST VIRGINIA

12/6   101.9 FM

Rules vary from game to game, so work it out before you start to play. Ex-WVU players are occasional participants, but it's a primarily under-graduate crowd.

COMMUNITY CENTER
JEFFERSON
SOUTH CHARLESTON, WEST VIRGINIA

6/3   950 AM

There's another slab outdoors, but the best games are run indoors, noonish and evenings during the winter. Games—to twelve by ones—are run straight if anyone's waiting.

ELKS PLAYGROUND
16TH AND MCCOLLOCH
WHEELING, WEST VIRGINIA

 4/2   97.3 FM

Set in the only black neighborhood in a predominantly white town, Elks attracts whites wanting to improve their games, and a solid corps of small-college regulars. A slam-bang tournament wraps up the pick-up season in late August.

WISCONSIN

ERB PARK
MORRISON AND PARKWAY
APPLETON, WISCONSIN

 2/1      1230 AM

A self-styled progressive community, this city has welcomed many of the Hmong, a.k.a. the Boat People. They have taken to hoop with gusto, and this is their chosen run.

FISH PARK
DOUSMAN
GREEN BAY, WISCONSIN

 2/1   101.1 FM

For cooling out (as if you need to in these parts), there's a swimming pool in the park and an ice-cream shop a block away. Winters, action moves (aren't we observant?) indoors, where school gyms open up for free play.

WEST YMCA
5515 MEDICAL CIRCLE
MADISON, WISCONSIN

6/3   104.1 FM

A unique facility where, a regular swears, complications, problems, and even disagreements do not arise.

HELFAER REC CENTER
MARQUETTE UNIVERSITY
MILWAUKEE, WISCONSIN

30/15      102.1 FM

With thirty hoops, you'd figure there wouldn't be much of a wait for nexts. Figure again: this spot "processes" as many as 1,000 players a day. A tad too many chumps; when new glass boards replaced the metal ones, one regular said, "It's like serving Dom Perignon to winos."

NORTH DIVISION COMMUNITY CENTER
1011 WEST CENTER
MILWAUKEE, WISCONSIN

14/7      102.1 FM

A tradition dating back to the '40s has made this the center-city place to play. South Division has a heavy Hispanic clientele. And drop in on the action at Mitchell Park on Milwaukee's South Side, where there's a great league on summer weekends.

HART PARK
7300 WEST CHESTNUT
WAUWATOSA, WISCONSIN

 10/5      102.1 FM

A middle-class game in a lowland just outside Milwaukee. The league is well run, even if most of the teams don't, by city standards, run well. Heed the wooden sign that urges players to WIN IF YOU CAN, LOSE IF YOU MUST, BUT PLAY THE GAME FAIR AND SQUARE.

Wauwatosa Twilight time is prime twine time at Hart Park. (Heinz Kleutmeier)

WYOMING

REC CENTER
EAST 4TH AND BEVERLY
CASPER, WYOMING

6/3

95.5 FM

The action here has picked up so much that hoopsters are now asked to get on a sign-up sheet if they wanna run.

HOLIDAY PARK
16TH AND MORRIE
CHEYENNE, WYOMING

4/2

100.7 FM

Holiday's back from a severe '85 flood that had ducks swimming around the rims. No lights, but with illumination from the adjacent horseshoe pitch—''and a full moon,'' says an insider—it's not too bad at night.

HALF ACRE
UNIVERSITY OF WYOMING
LARAMIE, WYOMING

6/3

103.9 FM

Yipee-yi-ay, yipee-yi-oh, pick-up hoops ranks second to the college rodeo. Watch out for cowboys, cowgirls, and cowpies.

213

THE THREE-UM
1021 SHERRY
RIVERTON, WYOMING

The Three-um because, with the rack set at 9', it's something short of the Forum. The court is fully marked, and two-on-two tournaments, with a smaller ball, are popular.

DISTRICT OF COLUMBIA

D.C.

"The Elgin Baylor Knee Situation really shook this town up," says Jim Wiggins, the capital fellow who founded and runs Washington's Urban Coalition League.

The Elgin Baylor Knee Situation: In D.C. they talk about it in grave tones, as if it were a Cuban Missile Crisis or Watergate. Indeed, as far as the city's hoop history is concerned, it was a watershed event. As a result of Baylor's disjointed joint, the most serious ball in this very serious city gets played indoors, on sheltered hardwood. Erstwhile outdoor hot spots have either fallen into desuetude, like Fort Stevens Park, or been flat out flattened, like the Chevy Chase Community Center court, which was razed years ago to make way for a new library. "Nobody," mused Red Auerbach on hearing that news, "went to the *old* library."

D.C. *A game of one-on-one is no grudge match at Friendship, which is greater Washington's Geneva.*

FRIENDSHIP REC CENTER
VAN NESS AND 45TH, N.W.
WASHINGTON, D.C.

 4/2    90.1 FM

The racial mix is a Room 222 casting director's dream: a white' hood with tidy facilities—including one long court—that attracts D.C.'s better bros. In fact, they stretch it out as soon as a quorum shows. The summer league runs Tuesdays and Thursdays; regular pick-up that's almost as good runs weekday mornings. This is D.C., and it is supervised by a guy named Bob Haldeman, but there's no truth to the rumor that you can't play unless you get taped.

JELLEFF BOYS AND GIRLS CLUB
WISCONSIN AND S, N.W.
WASHINGTON, D.C.

 2/1    90.1 FM

If you're eighteen or under, you can guest star for a day gratis. Otherwise, it's a good idea to join up, for the authorities card this fine slab. It's definitely a good idea to enlist if you want to run indoors, where there are six racks. The outdoor court is named after the late Dr. Michael Halberstam, brother of scribe David, who'd philanthropically hang nets from bare rims around this town.

MARTIN LUTHER KING REC CENTER
N AND DELAWARE, S.W.
WASHINGTON, D.C.

 2/1      96 FM

This spot in the Capitol Hill district gets up "once the sun goes down," as a regular says. Most of the leagues are for young'uns, the pick-up games for those longer in the tooth.

RAYMOND PLAYGROUND
10TH AND SPRING, N.W.
WASHINGTON, D.C.

2/1   96.3 FM

Stiff comp from a rough crowd. Spectators often gather to offer impromptu critiques of players' performances.

THE LAWNMOWER

Every city has him. He's the guy who can get a park teeming in minutes with just one well-placed phone call; will come crawling out of the woodwork at any event associated with the ten-foot culture; can find an inner-city innocent some tumbleweed-covered juco campus where he'll get a chance to *play.* No need to ask; they're smooth operators, and we've mentioned several of them—Detroit's Sam Washington, Houston's Angelo Cascio, and Lexington's Mel Cunningham—along the way. To move and shake with these men you have to pay your dues. Develop your style. Hone your wiles. So we went looking for the A number-1 power broker in the land, the *eminence grise* extraordinaire. He had to be someone whose devotion to the game stretched the limits. And we found D.C.'s Richard (The Lawnmower) Hicks a cut above.

Seems that one fine summer day several years back, Richard was intrigued by word of a local run. His wife, Olivia, thought the grass was getting a little long out back. She wanted him to cut the lawn. He wanted to go to the game. She was adamant. So, while Olivia was in the house, Richard took the mower out back. He revved it up. And he got in his car and went to the game.

Mower's still runnin'.

ASPHALT ARGOT

Ad	You've got the ad, or advantage, when you're one basket from victory. See also *deuce, game point, tight, up*.
Airball	A shot that touches neither rim, net, nor backboard. Also *house*.
All net	Nothing but bottom. Also *bic, scoop, string music, swish*.
Anchor	A shot likely to go "clang." Also *brick*.
Apple	The ball. Also *money, pill, rock*.
Around-the-world	A schoolyard shooting game in which players try to match each other shot-for-shot along an arc.
Ball	Basketball. To the hard core, the prefix "basket" is superfluous.
Bang	To hit the boards hard.
Bank's open	An interjection uttered while releasing a shot off the backboard. See also *board 'n' cord, knock-hockey player*.
Basketball Jones	On the street, a "jones" is an addictive habit. 'Nuf said.
Bic	This term for a successful shot that touches no iron is popular in the D.C.-Baltimore area. See also *all net, scoop, string music, swish*.
Blitz	To win a pick-up game in straight baskets, usually by 9-0. Also *skunk*.
The blocks	The low post, where *bounds* and *bunnies* can be had. Cf. *down low, underneath*.
Board 'n' cord	A shot banked off the backboard. See also *bank's open*.
Bogart	A strong move inside; **to Bogart** to make a strong move inside.
Boogie	To feint, fake, and ultimately score with a graceful move. Also *shake-'n'-bake, deal*.

219

Bound
Shorthand for rebound; **to bound** to rebound. Also *pull, snatch, yank.*

Bow
Shorthand for elbow; **to bow** to elbow.

Box
1. Portable stereo. A.k.a. ghetto blaster, Third World briefcase. 2. The foul lane. Also *crib, Death Valley, office, paint.*

Break the ice
The custom, common on some playgrounds, of not keeping score until at least one basket has been made.

Brick
A misfired shot with little chance of going in. Also *anchor.*

Bring it up
A command in a full-court game to inbound the ball. Also *take it out.*

Bro
Short for brother, which is short for soul brother.

Buckets
See *straight up.*

Bunny
See *chippie.*

Burn
1. To make a move that takes advantage of an opponent defensively. 2. To win convincingly. Also *school, use.*

Bush
Short for "bush league," as in dishonorable, gutless, or without class. A *submarine* is considered bush.

Bus stop
A jump shot. Also *J, joint.*

Bust
An explosive drive to the hoop.

Butcher
A physically abusive defensive player; **to butcher** to inflict physical punishment on another player. Also *hacker, hack.*

Camp
To establish position in the low post for extended periods of time. See also *play house.*

Can
To make a shot, usually from outside. Cf. *drain, drill, flush, trim.*

Change of hands
In half-court play, the rule requiring that the ball be brought back, usually to the foul line, after any change of possession, even after a steal, turnover, or *air ball.* Also *Washington.*

Check
1. A blocked shot. Frequently used synonyms include *gate, grill, hijack, rejection, snuff, stuff.* A shot hitting the bottom of the rim is sometimes called a *self-check.* 2. The defense's right to handle the ball *up top* or *out front* before it is inbounded, to be sure the *D* is ready; the practice of the defense handling the ball. Also *feel.* **to check** to block a shot.

Cherry picking	In a full-court game, the practice of laying back on defense to get a head start on a fast break. Also *snowbirding*.
Chicago	A *pick-up game* played to five by ones, with losers sitting.
Chinese basket	A shot that goes through the hoop, but enters and exits from the wrong sides. (It doesn't count.)
Chippie	An easy shot. Also *bunny*.
Chucker	See *gunner*.
Chump	Someone who can't play; the opposite of a *stud-fish*. As the bromide goes, the difference between "champ" and "chump" is "u." Also *Finkel, Janis Ian*.
City ball	See *straight up*.
Clearance	In a half-court game played according to *change of hands*, the ball must be cleared—brought *up top* or *taken around*—after a change of possession. *Side clearance* is fifteen to twenty feet away from the basket on the sides; *back clearance* is to the foul line or beyond.
Coast-to-coast	Baseline-to-baseline; full-court. Also *transcon*.
College style	See *winners*.
Comp	Competition. What—*ahem*—makes America great.
Count	The score.
Counterfeit	A shot with a dubious chance of going in.
Courtesy	During warm-ups, the custom of permitting a shooter to shoot until he misses. Rebounders aren't usually so chivalric for free throws, lay-ups, and short jumpers. Also *follows, rules of the court*.
CPR	A crowd pleaser.
Crew	A pick-up team. See also *house*.
Crib	The foul lane, after street talk for "house." Also *box, Death Valley, office, paint*.
Cup	See *rack*.
Cutting each other up	This is the best you can get in a pick-up game: two opponents, locked in man-to-man play, each outdoing the other's best. Face-to-face, so to speak.
D	Defense.
Day	White or whiteness, as in, "The dude's game is strictly *day*, man." Also *daytime, daylight*. Cf. *night*.
Deal	See *boogie*.
Death Valley	The foul lane. Also *box, crib, office, paint*.

Delay dunk	See *rub-in*.
Deuce	Playground *hoop* learned this from its more patrician cousin, tennis. Tie score, and you "gotta win by two." See also *ad, game point, tight, up*.
Dipsy-do	A short *double-pumped* shot, usually let go underhanded.
Dish	To pass off neatly; to make a deft pass, usually for an assist. Also *find, look*.
Doctor	A player who *operates* and makes *house calls*.
Do it	To make a strong, stylish maneuver on offense, in close quarters, or from the perimeter while being tightly guarded. Cf. *freak out, get back, operate, take it to him*.
Do or die	The ritual that determines who will get the first possession in a pick-up game. One player from one team takes a shot; if he makes it, his team takes the ball out. Also *hit or miss, make it, take it, shoot for the kill*.
Dog	See *rack*.
Double clutch	See *double pump*.
Double pump	A move that involves bringing the ball up and down after leaving your feet, yet still shooting it before traveling. Also *double clutch*.
Down	1. To have *winners*, or the next game; also known as *nexts*. 2. To be behind in the *count*. Cf. *up*.
Down low	See *underneath*.
Downtown	Way outside, where three-point shots are launched.
Drain	See *can*.
Drill	See *can*.
Drop-in	See *pick-up*.
Dunk	Surely you jest. Also *jam, slam, stuff, take, throwdown*. Cf. *funk dunk, punk dunk*.
D up	A call to play, or tighten up on, defense.
Eat it	See *taste that*.
Face	That intangible at stake in any man-to-man playground encounter that makes even single plays memorable. When it's at stake, one can do only one of two things: save it or lose it. Also *service*.
Face job	An individual offensive or defensive move so captivating that it wins for one moment the kharma of *face*. Also *facial, mug shot, Noxzema*.
Facial	See *face job*.

Fall back	See *scoot*.
Fats Domino	"He's walkin'." See also *take the train*.
Faye Dunaway	A fadeaway shot.
Feel	A *check*, usually *out front*.
Fill it up	To score on a succession of shots, usually from the outside.
Find	See *look*.
Finkel	Someone who can't play. After Henry Finkel, the robotlike former Celtic backup center. Also *chump*, *Janis Ian*.
Firsts	Without a referee, when two players tie each other up in what would otherwise be a jump ball, the player to yell "firsts" first gains possession. Cf. *shoot for it*.
Flush	To score. Cf. *toilet seater*.
Follows	See *courtesy*.
Freak out	With Fly McDuitt loose on the break, and only Sammy Suburban to beat to the goal, this is what someone in the gallery might yell. Cf. *do it, get back, operate, pay back, take it to him.*
Free ins	In cramped suburban driveways and city school-yards, half-court games are often played according to this principle: defenders may not intercept the first inbounds pass, nor may they harass the inbounder.
Free play	See *pick-up*.
Funk dunk	Any sort of *dunk* that showcases flair or leaping ability. Cf. *punk dunk*.
Game	With a possessive pronoun, indicates who's *down* or *up* for the next run ("It's my *game*"); or refers to a player's style ("His *game* is strictly left-hand"). Cf. *down, nexts, up, winners.*
Game point	The juncture in a game where one score can win it. Also *point game*. Cf. *ad, deuce, up.*
Garbage	A loose ball or rebound that results in a lay-up or short jumper. Cf. *Garbageman's Law, junk.*
Garbageman's Law	Backboard plus Spin equals Basket. Cf. *garbage, junk.*
Gate	See *check*.
Get back	1. To retreat on defense. 2. If you've been *burned* by an opponent, teammates or spectators will yell this and get you the ball so you can redeem yourself. Also *pay back*. Cf. *do it, freak out, operate, take it to him.*
Get burned	'Tis better to *burn* than *get burned*. Cf. *burn*.

Granny shot	An underhand free-throw.
Grease it	A cry heard from shooters whose shots are hanging on the rim.
Grill	See *check*.
Gunner	Someone who shoots a lot. Also *chucker, heaver, pump*.
Gusjohnson	To dunk so ferociously that rim is separated from backboard. (Ex-pro Gus Johnson did it once.) I *gusjohnson*, you *gusjohnson*, he *gusjohnsons*, we *gusjohnson*. "The basket be broke, 'cause he done *gusjohnsoned* it."
Gutbucket	Raw and untidy. A blues term, now used to describe the most engrossing type of schoolyard play.
Hacker	See *butcher*.
Handle	A player with good ball-handling skills is said to have a good *handle*.
Heaver	See *gunner*.
Hijack	See *check*.
Hit	A successful shot, usually banked in or taken at a low trajectory; **to hit** to make such a shot. Also *stick*.
Hit or miss	See *do or die*.
Hold court	To remain in successive pick-up games by virtue of consecutive victories. Cf. *winners*.
Hole	See *rack*.
Homeboy	Someone who shares your hometown or neighborhood is your *homeboy*. Cf. *man*.
Hood	Neighborhood.
Hoop	1. A scored basket. 2. The basket apparatus itself. 3. The game of basketball; also *hoops*. See also *ball*.
H-O-R-S-E	That most basic of playground diversions, in which each player must match the successful shot of any previous player. If your predecessor misses, you're free to shoot from anywhere. Anyone who misses after someone else's make is assessed a letter; spell H-O-R-S-E, and you are one. If life's hectic, just play P-I-G. See *match*.
House	1. A shot that touches nothing. See also *airball*. 2. A pick-up team stocked with talent. See also *crew*.
House call	A showy move, reserved for *doctors*. See also *operate*.
In your face	A phrase to be uttered after making a shot or de-

fensive play that humiliates an opponent. Also *in your eye, in your mug,* and (in such rare cases as a shot blocked with an elbow) *in your neck.*

The J	The jump shot. Also *bus stop, joint.*
Jam	See *dunk.*
Janis Ian	Someone who can't play. After the woman who penned the line, "Those whose names were never called when choosing sides for basketball." Also *chump, Finkel.*
Joint	See *The J.*
Jones	See *Basketball Jones.*
Juke	A sudden move used by either an offensive or defensive player, usually as a decoy. May be part of *wheeling and dealing* or a defensive ploy.
Junk	An awkward or unusual shot not normally in a shooter's repertoire; sometimes even *garbage.*
Kentucky rules	See *straight up.*
Kicks	Sneakers. Also *tread.*
Knock-hockey player	A bank-shot artist. Cf. *bank's open.*
Light	See *PT.*
Lincoln	See *straight up.*
Li'l help	The playground S.O.S. If your ball rolls away toward a neighboring game or gets stuck in a tangled chain net, this alerts others that you'd like them to retrieve it, or offer their ball so you can jar yours free. (Whatever you do, though, don't utter the annoyingly presumptuous "Thank you!" that's heard around country clubs.) Bill Murray (in *Stripes*) yells "Li'l help!" to a passerby after Murray has mistakenly thrown a ball out the window of his living room *cum* basketball court. The ball comes flying back a few moments later.
Load up	The technique of manipulating the *pick-up* process to give your team an edge. Also *stack.*
Look	A pass, usually inside, that leads to a basket. Also *dish, find.*
Losers	In half-court ball, the system in which possession reverts to the defending team after a basket. Cf. *make it, take it, winners.*
Make it, take it	See *winners;* also see *do or die.*
Man	1. An opponent who's being guarded. 2. Shorthand for man-to-man defense. 3. A protégé or

	teammate. To be called "my main man" is preferable to merely "my man." Cf. *homeboy*.
Match	This principle is invoked to settle a dispute, or to decide who'll play when there's a surplus of players. If the first shooter hits, his counterpart must match the shot; otherwise, possession or the right to play belongs to the first shooter. The basis of the game of H-O-R-S-E. See also *H-O-R-S-E*. Cf. *shoot for it*.
Meminger's Law	An edict promulgated by former pro and New York playground habitué Dean Meminger. It holds that, if you don't play ball, you can't hang out.
Mombo	A series of head, shoulder, or ball fakes.
Money	See *rock*.
Mug shot	See *face job*.
My bad	An expression of contrition, uttered after making a bad pass or missing an assignment.
Nab	See *zebra*.
Nag	A coach. Most nags'll nag you for whipping it behind the back.
New York	See *straight up*.
Nexts	See *winners*.
Night	Black or blackness, as in, "Check out the *night* in my *man*'s moves." Also *sundown*. Cf. *day*.
Noxzema	See *face job*.
Office	See *crib*.
Operate	To *do it* in close quarters. A technique not taught in med schools. Cf. *do it, doctor, freak out, house call, take it to him*.
Out front	The area beyond the foul line where, in half-court play, the ball is *checked* before being "inbounded." Also *up top*.
Outs	The right to inbound the ball.
Paint	See *crib*.
Palm	1. To hold the ball in one hand, usually for show. Obligatory for most varieties of *funk dunk*. 2. The illegal dribble on which there's no prohibition in the speakeasies of the schoolyard.
Pay back	See *get back*.
Pearl	A move you wouldn't be ashamed to take uptown. Believers in the Earl Monroe Doctrine may throw in a spin and some *wheeling and dealing*.

Pick-up	Unorganized ball. *Pick-up game, pick-up team.* Also *drop-in, free play, ratball.*
Pill	See *rock.*
Play house	To establish dominance *underneath.*
Point game	See *game point.*
Pop	A suddenly released jumper; **to pop** to shoot suddenly.
Possession	See *winners.*
Prayer	A shot let go in such desperation that it seems only divine intervention will put it in the basket.
PT	Playing time. Also *light.*
Pull	See *bound.*
Pump	See *gunner.*
Punk dunk	A sort of *dunk* in which the dunker attempts to humiliate the dunkee. Cf. *funk dunk.*
Push it up	Yell this when you want the ball to be brought quickly into the forecourt.
Rack	The basket. Also *cup, dog, hole.*
Rain	A succession of successful shots, usually from the outside.
Ratball	See *pick-up.*
Rat race	A high-scoring game.
Rattle	A successful shot in which the ball hits the inside of the rim several times before dropping through. Cf. *drill, hit, pop, rip, stick, swish.*
Rejection	See *check.*
Rep	Reputation.
Ride	Car. Your ride's battery and headlights sometimes come in handy when you want to play at night.
Rip	A successful shot, usually a *swish.* Cf. *drill, hit, pop, rattle, stick, swish.*
Rise	See *sky.*
Rock	The ball. Also *apple, money, pill.*
Rockfish	Someone who can play. Term popularized by— and named after—shadowy hoops talent scout Ian Rockfish. See also *studfish.*
Rub-in	A dunk attempt that isn't quite accomplished cleanly, yet still results in the ball passing through the hoop. Also *delay dunk.*
Rules of the court	See *courtesy.*
Run	A full-court *pick-up game;* **to run** to play full-court *ball.* Has nothing to do with jogging.

227

Run a clinic	1. To execute a play crisply. 2. To win convincingly.
Run it back	The request of a *pick-up team* that has just been beaten to get an immediate rematch. If another team has *winners* or *nexts,* the request won't be granted.
Run 'n' gun	Fast-break *ball.*
School	To take advantage of someone by pulling a deft offensive move. Also *burn, use.*
Scoop	See *swish.*
Scoot	A player's call to his teammates to retreat, or scoot back, on defense because he knows his shot's going in. Also *fall back.*
Self-check	See *check.*
Sell wolf tickets	See *woof.*
Send it	You'll hear this cry from a *cherry picker* who wants a rebounding teammate to let go an outlet pass.
Service	See *face.*
Sewer	A basket so loose that anything going near it goes down it.
Shake	To elude an opponent, usually by duping him with a stutterstep or *juke,* and then breaking away.
Shake 'n' bake	See *boogie.*
Shirts	See *shirts 'n' skins.*
Shirts 'n' skins	The schoolyard's uniforms. One team plays shirtless for easier identification. Still hasn't been met with wide acceptance among women.
Shoot for it	The shooting of fingers, or the shooting of a shot, to decide who'll get possession when a jump ball or other quandary arises. Cf. *match, the line don't lie.*
Shoot for the kill	See *do or die.*
Sidecar	A player who can *rise* so readily that he seems to put the ball on his hip, as if it were a sidecar, before *jamming.* The nickname of legendary *skywalker* Jackie Jackson.
Skins	See *shirts 'n' skins.*
Skunk	To win a pick-up game in straight baskets, usually by 9-0. Also *blitz.*
Sky	Not merely to jump, but to sail—in pursuit of *hoops, bounds, rejections,* or just a whiff of rarer air. Also *rise, talk to God.*

Skywalk	An aerial stroll; **to skywalk** to go for a stroll at rim level.
Slab	The court, usually asphalt. See also *wood*.
Slam	See *dunk*.
Snatch	See *bound*.
Snowbirding	*Cherry picking* in the South.
Snuff	See *check*.
Stack	See *load up*.
Stick	See *hit*.
Straight	You don't have to win by two when you play according to this method of scoring. Cf. *deuce*.
Straight up	Half-court ball, played according to the rule that any rebound or turnover can be shot immediately, without *clearing* the ball, or *taking it around*. Also *buckets, city ball, Kentucky rules, Lincoln, New York*.
Stretch it out	To run full court. If you've been playing three-on-three at one hoop and four guys suddenly show up, someone may say, "Let's *stretch it out*." Cf. *coast-to-coast, transcon*.
String music	Sportscaster Joe Dean's term for a shot that bottoms out. Also *all net, bic, scoop, swish*.
Stroke	Shot or shooting motion. Larry Bird has a stroke of genius. Also *tick*.
Studfish	Someone who can play. See also *rockfish*.
Stuntman	Someone who when fouled exaggerates the extent of the contact.
Stuff	1. See *dunk*. 2. See *check*.
Submarine	To undercut a player who has left his feet on the way to the *hole*. It's *bush*.
Sundown	See *night*. Cf. *day*.
Swish	A successful shot that passes through the hoop without hitting rim or backboard. Also *all net, bic, scoop, string music*.
Tailor	Someone not only deft at blocking shots, but at altering them, too.
Take	See *dunk*.
Take it around	To bring the ball into the backcourt in a half-court game played according to *change of hands*. Also *take it back*.
Take it back	See *take it around*.
Take it out	To inbound the ball. Also *bring it up*.

Take it to him	A suburban rendering of the more urban *do it* or *freak out*.
Takers	See *winners*.
Take the train	A less-than-diplomatic suggestion that someone has traveled. Variations include "Take the A Train" (New York), "Take the El" (Chicago), "Take the Amtrak," "Take the Greyhound," and the ever-discreet "I believe I heard the pitter-patter of little feet." See also *Fats Domino*.
Talk to God	See *sky*.
Taste that	After blocking an opponent's shot, say this to remind him of what he can do with it. Also *eat it*.
Tending	Goaltending. When in the *office*, one often *tends* to affairs.
The line don't lie	See *shoot for it*.
Three-sixty	A shot off a drive in which the shooter spins 360 degrees between the time he takes off and lands, yet still lets a shot go. Also *whirlybird*.
Throwdown	See *dunk*.
Tick	Shot. To get *a good tick goin'* is to be on a shooting roll. Also *stroke*.
Tight	Tied. If a game's being played straight to fifteen and someone yells out "fourteen tight," it's time to play ball. Also *up*.
Toilet seater	A shot that rolls around the rim several times before dropping through or spinning out. Also *victory lap*. Cf. *flush*.
Too late	Cocky shooters utter this as they let their J's go, to let a defender know he's been tardy in coming by to *snuff* the shot.
Transcon	See *coast-to-coast*.
Trash	1. To make use of the *Garbageman's Law*. 2. When you beat a host *pick-up team*, you can boast of having *trashed* their court.
Tread	See *kicks*.
Tree	A tall player.
Trim	To make a shot. Also *can, drain, drill, flush*.
Tude	Attitude.
Twine	Net. Root for the expressions *twine time* and *twine twinkler*.
Underneath	The area along the baseline, under the basket, where *doctors operate*. Also *down low*.

Up	1. All; with a number, indicates that the score is tied. Also *tight;* cf. *ad, deuce, game point.* 2. A person or team claiming the next game is said to be up. Cf. *down, winners.* 3. To be in the lead.
Up top	See *out front.*
Use	See *school.*
Victory lap	See *toilet seater.*
Washington	See *change of hands.* Cf. *Lincoln.*
Western Union	The telegraphing of a pass or a shot so that a steal or block results.
Wheel	Ankle. A bad *wheel* can hamper a *skywalker.*
Wheeling 'n' dealing	See *deal.*
Whirlybird	See *three-sixty.*
White man's disease	A chronic inability to jump. Sometimes referred to as "the dread disease."
Wing	Arm. A bad wing can hamper a good shooter.
Winners	1. The system of inbounding that lets the scoring team retain possession of the ball after a basket. Also *college style, make it, take it, possession, takers.* 2. A player waiting calls this to get *down* for the next game, usually against the winning, defending team. Also *nexts.*
Wood	The court. Short for hardwood, but applies to all surfaces. Also *slab.*
Woof	To address an opponent in an intimidating fashion. Also *sell wolf tickets.*
Yank	See *bound.*
You	An exhortation one player will make to a teammate, encouraging him to take a shot or make a move.
Zebra	1. A referee. 2. A player who thinks he's a ref and calls everything. Also *nab.*
Zilch	See *zip.*
Zip	A score of zero. Also *zilch.*
Zoom	To defend.

ABOUT THE AUTHORS

CHUCK WIELGUS lives on Hilton Head Island, S.C., where he is executive director of the Hilton Head Island Recreation Association. A 1972 graduate of Providence College, he has coached basketball at the high school and college levels. Look for Chuck at the Courthouse Annex (p. 180).

ALEXANDER WOLFF graduated from Princeton University in 1980 and is currently a writer on the staff of *Sports Illustrated*. He has played amateur basketball in Switzerland and now makes his home in New York City. Look for Alex at the Vanderbilt Y (p. 139).

Chuck and Alex are coauthors of *The In-Your-Face Basketball Book*.